“The Day That ([illegible] To Visit My Garden”

(A Fiction title by Sandra Embleton)

Kim,

Spirit walks tall
in those who up hold
the laws of Spirit...

Walk On ....

Sandra Embleton.

Disclaimer

Before you embark upon this amazing adventure into the world of the spirit, know this"

Oprah, has no knowledge of me, nor of this book. Nor does she endorse it or recommend it. I was lead to write it as an imaginary interview. I did call upon her energy and her spirit to assist in its telling.

I tried my best however, to email her and ask her for permission to use her name last year and got no response.

My intention was never to capitalize on the use of Oprah's name, but rather to follow spirit's guidance in the telling of this tale.

Thank-you

Sandra Embleton
2285 Dunedin Road
Oakville, Ontario
L6J5V4
Email: sandra_embleton@yahoo.ca

Dedication

This work of spiritual art is dedicated to our Father God, who works mightily through One of His Greatest Lights, Oprah Winfrey.

The Day That Oprah Came To Visit My Garden

As far back as I can remember, I have always wanted to be on the Oprah Winfrey Show. I have grown up believing that is the place to be if you have some incredible ability, some life altering discovery, a message to give to the world, or if you have lost a lot of weight.

It is the place where those of us who have climbed incredible mountains, or have overcome impossible obstacles gather to share our journey's in the hope that by doing this, we may, in some small way, ease the burden somewhat, of those who are on a similar path. We come to share and we watch so that we can learn. We watch so that no matter what our plight, we may have hope.

That's what Oprah does for us. She brings us all together and she gives us hope.

Amazing Oprah!

I have climbed incredible mountains. I have overcome impossible obstacles. God has placed in me, an incredible message to deliver to the world. My message from God to us all is that it is time to go Home.

I have a small problem.

I don't know how to get on the Oprah show to deliver it. Naturally, I think of going on the Oprah show because that is the place where messages such as mine are customarily delivered.

It’s a place where I can safely tell every one of my life's work.
You see, God has also given me the access code to The Garden of Eden.

If I can share it with the world, others will be able to gain access to The Garden and as a result, walk with God.

My amazing abilities are that I am able to know God. The reason that I can state this is because it is God who chose to share Himself with me for a three week period in February of 94. During this time, I was able to speak with Him and have Him answer many questions that I had of Him. I was able to let Him enter into me and have a look around at His marvelous creations from a human pair of eyes. We developed quite a love for one another during that encounter and it sticks with me, even to this day.

I kept thinking for many years that this was a normal occurrence and that others in the world would be able to share in this knowledge of God with me. So, far, I have found very few.

Recently, I found evidence of this kind of God-knowing in Deepak Chopra's new book, "A Third Jesus". What freedom is found in those pages! Is it any wonder, in a past lifetime, Deepak once walked the earth as an actual disciple of Jesus? How can I make that claim? Well, you see, among the many gifts bestowed upon me by God, one of them is the ability to know who it is that people once walked the earth as, in previous lifetimes. What it is that they are here to do, and how it is that they must proceed?

It's quite a lot to let out in just a one hour show.

So, I asked God how it is that He would like this message delivered to His people and He opted out for the old fashioned way… "Let Moses do it" -- which suits me just fine; I really don't have the people's ear any ways.

So, with my objective somewhat clearer, I found a way to give birth to the spirit of God once again upon the earth by delivering my message to someone who would be able to carry it to all the people.

That someone is you Oprah.

In case you are not yet aware of whom it is that you are - you are the one chosen by God to deliver this message to your people. You are in fact carrying the energy of Moses. It is through you that this information will come to light upon the world.

I am simply the one who will tell you what that message is this: It’s time to be heading Home -- Home to oneness with God.

“But it's how to do it” the Wicked Witch of the West ponders as she is scratching her chin.

My next obvious move: invite Oprah to visit me and I will show her my Garden of Eden!

Problem: What are the chances of her accepting?

100% after she reads this book!

So, I will write an imaginary meeting between Oprah and myself. In this meeting, I will do my best to channel what it is that Oprah might say and how it is that she would react.

I will do my best to channel what it is that God would have Oprah and my readers know. I will then further use this venue to release my findings and my discoveries so that at least they will have been recorded, if not believed.

Now for your enjoyment, your enlightenment I give to you all…

The Day That Oprah Came To Visit My Garden

Chapter One: Introductions

My son was waiting at the airport for Oprah and her best friend. I knew that if I were to get Oprah all the way out here to visit my Garden, that there was no way that Gayle was going to let her go to some stranger's cottage by herself. After all, she's Oprah! She needs an escort where ever she goes -- and, rightly so. Also, being Oprah's best friend, well, there would be a certain amount of love and concern for one's friend's safety that should not and will not be taken lightly.

I already like Gayle, even though we have yet to meet. So, I invited her too! Just not into The Garden. She was to come along so far and then stay with my family while I was being interviewed by Oprah. This was no hardship as my other son was in charge of entertaining Gayle. You see my son was recently enrolled in the Stand-Up Comedy, Writing and Performance Program offered at a local college. He is most likely the fastest rising comedic talent his school and local comedy clubs have yet to produce. Spoken like a proud mother! Gayle will be given the royal treatment and the worst that could happen to her is that she will leave with her sides hurting from laughing so hard.

After dropping Gayle off, Oprah proceeded north also being pleasantly entertained by her chauffeur, Doug (my other son). Oprah had many questions regarding me and my family, which Doug did his level best to answer during the course of their drive. After the short hour and a half, she finally arrived at our cottage. We have rented the same cottage now for about seven or eight years. It just happens to be located right beside the one that I grew up in as a little girl.

I was anxiously waiting for her at the end of the driveway as Doug had called me with an accurate time of arrival.

I had to admit, I was nervous. Imagine… Oprah was actually coming herself, in person to meet me and to see with her own eyes my Garden of Eden.

No cameras, no film crew, just Oprah and me.

I was just hoping that the interview would go well and that she would be as happy to finally meet me as I was her. I mean the stuff that I was about to share with her was quite a lot to take in. I had to remind myself that I had been working on all this for the past twenty years and to try and give it all to this woman in a few hours would be information overload. I would just have to trust that whatever was to come out would come out and that everything was going to be just fine.

I could see the car approaching. I said an out loud prayer to God, "Please Lord, I'm going to put this one in your hands! Just give me the courage to allow your truth to flow through me so that you may be heard."

I could see the car approaching. Dave let us borrow his Cadillac for the day so that she would at least have a comfortable ride up here. Doug was more than happy to do the driving.

The car pulled in and I was there to open the door for her,
"Hello, hello, well I see you made it up here safely in one piece!" I said to Oprah as she swung her legs out and made it to her feet.
"Lordy, Lordy, that was a long drive let me get out here and just stretch my legs!"

"Welcome, Oprah" I smiled and with that opened my arms to greet her properly.

I gave her a customarily acceptable hug upon a first time greeting. I wanted to convey to her our warmth and that she was with family and in safe hands.

“Look at this beautiful place” she commented as she removed her sunglasses to get a better look around.

Before we knew it, Doug was bringing around Oprah's bag and carrying it up to the cottage.

“I'm glad that you took my advice and packed your bathing suit and an overnight bag, just in case.”

“Always good to be prepared” she returned.

We walked up towards the cottage.

“It's not much to look at,” I explained and then continued,
“It's just a cottage, but it suits us fine. It gives us what we need. After all, I'm outside almost all of the time up here.”

Oprah walked with me up the lawn and then exclaimed,
“Is that the Garden?” pointing right to it.

“Yes, Oprah, as a matter of fact it is.”

We both crossed over to the Garden's entrance and I heard her gasp.

“It's beautiful, just beautiful!” “It is, isn't it?” I smiled and swelled with pride.

“May we go in?” she asked me.

“Yes, we may. However before you enter, there are some things that I would like to share with you. I was hoping that we would sit and talk for awhile over on the patio.” And I pointed in that direction as I continued to inform her.

“That way we could get to know one another a little bit better and I am sure that you’re needing to use the facilities as well as have something to eat and drink."

"You read my mind Sandra!" she reached out and placed her arm around me and we walked up to the cottage.

"Oprah, this cottage that we rent is among the first to be built along this beach. It was originally constructed in 1955, the year of my birth. It is basic and decorated like Nate's worst nightmare" and we both had a laugh at that comment as Oprah turned to look at me and said.

"Nate has seen his fair share of challenges Sandra." I in turn raised my eyebrows and uttered, "Well, then this surely would be one of them!"

It was true, although I was somewhat embarrassed with regards to my lowly accommodations, I offered no apologies. Heaven is where you find it. And now, I was going to share my piece of heaven with Oprah herself! After all, Oprah didn't come here to see the cottage; she came here to see me and to visit my Garden. I ushered her up towards the patio and asked if she would make herself to home as I went inside to get the lunch I had prepared for us to enjoy.

We both ate and managed to exchange pleasantries while we partook in our mid-day meal. I had made lemonade and my Mother's peanut butter, onion, mayonnaise, lettuce, salt and pepper sandwiches. Hey! Don't knock it until you have tried them! Served on fresh bread with pickles and pickled eggs, why it's a lunch fit for a queen! Fit for Oprah!

Our conversation began.

"Thanks for hauling yourself all the way up here to meet with me to hear my story." I found myself saying. She responded with, "Well, you can't write a book like you did without getting everyone's attention. I just want to know if it's true or not."

"Sandra, what you are saying about 2012? There is so much gloom and doom being speculated with regards to this change in times. I want to believe what you are telling us is true, because quite frankly, when I read about your thoughts, it made me feel wonderful. More than that, I want to experience what it is that you have said you had experienced."

Then, she paused, took in a nice long breath of fresh air and looked around at her new surroundings and added, "Up here, in this beautiful place."

"I know you do, and, if you are meant to, Oprah, you will. I have no control over what will happen here. It is all up to the Big Guy upstairs." And I pointed my finger upwards.

"But I do know that. He asked me to tell you all about it, so here goes".

"I would ask you though, do not try to write things down that you are about to hear, just try to be in the moment and try to experience this for yourself Oprah. I really want you to feeeeellll this day and all that you are about to witness. For it is God Himself that has called you to this place and I am simply His voice. I take no responsibility for the outcome of this day, be it good or bad. However, I have been at this spiritual stuff for quite awhile now and I can safely say that I am pretty sure that God wouldn't have called you all the way up here to let you go home empty-handed." And I gave her a thumbs-up signal and forewarned her.

"So, hang onto your hat girlfriend because this is going to be the ride of your life!" And I sat back in my chair and asked spirit.

"Now, where to begin?" I smiled upon receiving guidance and then reached over and took Oprah's hand. I began by taking in a few deep breaths and I said, "I'm just going to have a short prayer. We both closed our eyes and began to breath.

“Father, I have done as you have asked of me and invited Oprah to your Garden, would you please be with us this day and would you guide us. Allow us to feel your presence. Come to us through nature and through signs. Fill us with your spirit and your knowing, so that we may be close to you and hear your voice. I ask this of you Oh Lord. Thank you.”

We opened our eyes.

Chapter Two

"That was lovely." Oprah smiled.

"Oprah, I have been working for the past twenty years at getting to know God. Getting to know the world of spirit and how it operates. That is what I would like to share with you today, what it is that I have learned about the world of spirit. I can remember you stating on one of your shows that a book should be in two parts. The first part, a) this is who I am, and the second part b) this is what I know."

"Yes, I believe I did say something to that effect, didn't I? Humph."

"Oprah, it is because of who it is that I am, that my message is of such importance. And I will stress this immediately; I first had to learn who it was that I am."

"And who are you?"

"I am God's messenger." And I paused to smile as I then added "and a very old soul."

"You're telling me that God speaks to you and gives you information?"

"Which in turn, I record in a journal."

"Like a secretary or something?"

With that I held out my hands and took Oprah's in mine and I began to laugh.

"Yes, that is exactly what I mean. I have been writing for God for the past twenty or so years. He and I have had a relationship that has been both supernatural and fantastical!" and with that I smiled a beautiful smile, paused and shook my head from side to side.

"Oprah, the world where we live is not what it appears to be. There is more going on than you can imagine at any given time. And hear this: it is all perfectly laid out for us. The only time we get into trouble is when we try to interfere with the plan."

"How is it that we can interfere with God's plan if everything is so perfectly planned out?"

"We do this by thinking there is something wrong with the way things are, and we then commence to spend our energy trying to 'fix' things."

"Like what?"

"Like when we try to fix friends, family and ourselves for one thing. Thinking there is something wrong with the way things are moves us into the doing and the fixing, rather than living with acceptance of what is God's will for us. God wants us to spend our time here on this earth loving one another and seeking Him out. The trick is in order to come to know and love God you must first begin to love yourself. This sets you on the road to knowing God."

Oprah was shaking her head up and down in such a manner as I believe she was taking in what I was sharing with her.

"Oprah, in order to begin to seek out God, you must first seek out a quiet place of your own to just "Be" with Him."

Then I turned and gestured for Oprah to look around at her new surroundings.

"See down there in that beautiful grove, where my hammock is hanging?”

“Yeah.” And Oprah turned somewhat if her chair and looked where I was pointing.

“That is my place to be with God. Can you imagine a more beautiful place in which you can just ‘Be’?”

Oprah looked and took in a deep breath as she surveyed the premises.

“It is so beautiful.” Oprah agreed by moving her head up and down in an affirmative gesture. She then asked me.

“Sandra, by just “Being”, what is it you mean by that?”

“It means not to do, but to rest and be still. It is only when one is rested and still that God can enter in. The Bible teaches us this.”

“Yeah. I still can’t figure out myself how a concept so simple can be so powerful.”

“That’s just it, it is so simple. We make it hard by avoiding the ‘being’ and replacing it with the ‘got to be doing’. We constantly drive ourselves further from a relationship with God by the got to be moving, making, fixing, changing, always working, striving to be better kind of world the majority of us have agreed to live in. Take for example, your coming up here to this part of the country Oprah. The majority of the local residents are farmers and farm people. The difference in the energy that is produced in this place verses the energy that exists in our cities is quite remarkable.”

“You mean it is calmer up here and people are more relaxed and friendly?”

I looked at Oprah with a look that displayed how impressed I was with that answer and then said to her, “Yeah, that’s exactly what I mean. How did you know that?"

"I could feel it. On the way up here your son and I made a stop and I got to talk to some of the people from around here."

"Really?" I lit up. Then she continued.

"I got a sense from them that they were genuine in their asking about me and my well-being. You know, they weren't after anything from me. Just happy to meet with me."

"I think it the energy comes from people being closer to nature and being with the land." I responded and continued on. "We have a lot to learn from the farmers."

"I agree with you there Sandra. But we can't all become farmers."

"No, but we can all spend time in nature and be on the land. We can also begin to seek out finding places in nature that we can create a safe space to just begin to 'Be'".

"Such as your Garden?"

"Such as my Garden." And here I made a sweeping hand gesture towards it.

"When we take time to just 'Be', you know, just sit or lay down quietly somewhere, God will speak to us. And He does this through the energy which is called His Holy Spirit."

"So the Holy Spirit is kind of like a messenger?"

"Yes. And when this energy delivers a message to you, there is no mistaking it. No guessing what so ever. It is instantaneous and it fills your entire being."

"From head to toe?"

"From head to toe!" I echoed back to her.

"Really? You can actually feel the Holy Spirit?"

"I believe that you can, because it has happened to me."

"So, how does it make you feel?"

"I felt strong and full of purpose."

"So, you're telling me that if I take time in my Garden, I will hear the voice of God and He will tell me what I am to be doing?"

"Like a GPS?" Oprah queried.

"Yes Oprah!" I laughed out loud at the comparison she had chosen to use.

"It is exactly like a GPS."

"Wow. That is good to know. So, Sandra, the presence of God and of spirit is getting more and more forceful?"

"Exactly, Oprah. There is a world outside of, yet existing simultaneously with the physical world that we are all familiar with. It is the world of the spirit. The world of the spirit is one that can make sense of who it is that we are and what it is that we are here to do. The problem for many, if not all of us, is that the steps it takes to access this world are not ones that everyone chooses to follow. Remember, in the Bible we get a clue that the road to God is wide, but the path is narrow? It means that access to God's spirit is for us all, but few choose to follow it to the end. Well, Oprah, I have followed that narrow pathway to the end and I am here to tell you that it truly does lead to God. It leads us right back to the beginning of the Bible. It takes us right back into the Garden of Eden and into an open and equal exchange with God. Just like it was in the beginning IS now until the end because the pathway is always open and we can choose to return Home any time that we wish to!"

"How can I access this pathway? Sandra, tell me that" she said. The secret to accessing the pathway is to begin to gain access into yourself. The more that you get to know about yourself, the more you will get to know God. It truly is a magical code Oprah."

Oprah looked at me, scrunching up her forehead. I got from that signal that she was not getting a clear picture. I continued onto explain.

"Start from now and work backwards into your childhood. Learn as much as you can about yourself and your life right back into your childhood and along the way, you will begin to meet up with God. Are you aware that when you are in that place of rescue and recovery of the wounded inner child that you are in the valley?"

Oprah looked puzzled.

"The valley?" she questioned.

"Yes, the valley of the shadow of death that we hear about in Psalm #23. That is the route you must pass through."

"Are you telling me that we pass through that valley when we are alive in life? I thought that it was God watching over us when we die?"

"I believe that it actually refers to is the time in your life when you do die."

"What do you mean?" Oprah quickly asked me.

"You die to your concept of your old self. When you begin to release your past held views that you have needed to hold onto in order to survive your childhood, and even into your adulthood. It refers to the time on our healing journey towards the rescue and recovery of the dead self. It is how we come to be born again. Oprah, I have learned that when we arrive here, perfect and innocent in our being, within a short time, we enter into Hell. How we do this is when that innocent spirit that we bring here with us is violated. Either emotionally, physically or sexually. Our sense of self and our ability to trust unconditionally is removed from us. Once our innocence is removed, our yellow brick road, so to speak, is the setting out and searching for our missing children. Our lost connection to the 'All that Is'. You die to your real self, which is the knowledge that you are part of God. The curse is that we forget that. The horror of it is that we don't even remember that we have lost it!! Welcome to crazy land! You might as well take your seat at 'The Mad Hatter's Tea Party' and get ready not to have anything make any sense at all! Oprah, the madness is that it is all madness!"

"Sandra that is a pretty good description of Hell." Oprah concurred as she was shaking her head up and down, lips pressed tightly together.

"I guess the point I really just want to make is that as troubled as some of our past histories may be, it is all a necessary evil. It's necessary, because it happens. God would not allow it if it were not meant for our higher learning."

"So, rather than being angry or revengeful, acceptance helps you to come to a place of letting go and getting on with the healing?"

"Exactly. We are here to be in that evil and to find our way back."

"Back to our innocence?"

“Yes, and to the heart to heart connection that exists between us and the One who created us.”

Oprah took in a big sigh. I continued on.

“Evil is with us, as is God. The evil that we all must face is the evil that exists within our own minds!”

“Hello ego!” Oprah chimed in.

“Precisely. It follows us wherever we go!”

“Cause our brains go where we go!” Oprah cited.

“Got to learn to love it! Our egos remain strong as long as we refuse to look at them. The moment that we choose to face that nagging inner voice and challenge its critical messages, we can begin to find inner peace.”

“So this is a prerequisite in order to walk on the path?”

“Yes, I'm afraid it is. What helped me to understand how harmful my ego could be, was to begin to count throughout my day, the number of hurtful or negative thoughts I was thinking to myself.”

“You mean when we choose to focus on a meeting that didn’t go right?”

“Or a conversation with a friend or relative that turned into an argument.”

“Ooo! I know that feeling. Sometimes I go over and over again in my mind what had just transpired.”

“Almost hoping that if you replayed it again and again the outcome may have been different?”

“Yes!” and here Oprah turned and pointed her finger right at me and then at her head as she continued on with.

“It just keeps on repeating and repeating in my mind and it keeps on making me feel badly, every time I play it over again! It’s so hard to shake it!”

“Next time you find your mind constantly going back to an incident that causes you upset, try using the Ho’oponopono words.”

“The Ho’opp…onop words?”

“Yes, four phrases that when recited in your mind help to clear out the negative ego’s thoughts. They also help to heal the exact situation that you are upset with.”

“Really Sandra?”

“Yes.”

“Well, what are the words that you are supposed to say?”

“Simply say I’m sorry, please forgive me, thank-you, I love you.”

“I’m sorry.” Oprah began to recite after me then slowly, searching for the words added.

“Please forgive me.” Then I jumped in as she began to hesitate with the last two phrases.

“Thank-you.” And then the two of us recited simultaneously.

“I love you!” We both smiled at one another.

“Try it! I try to say it in my mind as much as I can throughout the day.

"That's a lot Sandra!"

"Not really once you get the hang of it."

"Why so often?"

"Because it is cleaning away past hurts and thought patterns."

"It that so?"

"That is so."

"Well, my, my. Where did you hear about this?"

"A girlfriend of mine learned it from a Hawaiian doctor. Doctor Hew Len I believe."

"And she told you about it?"

"Yup. And I have been practicing it ever since. It's really a powerful tool for all of us to use Oprah."

"I'll remember that Sandra. Maybe I can do a special on this if the good doctor would agree to be my guest."

"You never know until you ask."

Chapter Three

"Oprah, do you remember the movie, The Wizard of Oz?"

"Yes, I do!" she lit up. "One of my childhood favorites."

"Mine too!" I agreed, and then continued on.

"The reason that movie was so important is because it is a Modern day contribution channeled by Frank L. Baum from God to gently point out the narrow road that leads us Home."

Judging by the look on Oprah's face, I knew that further explanation was required.

"Think back upon the movie. It is about a girl, Dorothy, who with her dog Toto, (God spelled backwards) was discontent with her life. She wanted to be in a place 'Somewhere over the Rainbow'. When she landed in that place, she was introduced to both the good and the evil that existed there by representation of the Witches of the North and the West. Her main goal was to find her way Home. Just like our main goal is! We are here to get back to the beginning. To find our way back Home to God. Remember Oprah, in the movie when she was surrounded by the Munchkins, they represent children, our childhood. Dorothy exclaims as she places her ruby red slipper at the very tip of the beginning of the yellow brick road that "It is always best to start at the beginning"? It was not just a casual comment - it was a very big clue on how to get to the land of OZ. Heaven. The beauty of the movie and in our own lives is that you don't have to die to do it!"

"What?" she bellowed.

"Are you telling me that you do not have to die to get to Heaven?"

“Yes, yes! I am! That is what is so great about my discovery into the Garden of Eden. Look, Oprah, what is the Garden of Eden anyways?” I asked her.

She pondered and then laughed a bit, before answering.

“Well” she said, “I guess it’s Paradise.”

“That's right - it is, and according to what we are told in the Bible, what is the accurate description of Paradise?”

“Will Smith.” I just went silent for a moment because the answer she gave was so unexpected. Then, the silence broke and we both just howled at this together.

“Oprahhhhh. You devil you!”

“That’s right girl! Uh Ah! I be bad.”

“For sure you are with that last one!” We laughed again and after a few moments, calmed down again, Oprah then said in a more serious tone.

“It's about being safe and protected. Totally cared for by God.”

“You’re absolutely right! What else do we know? We know that God comes and goes in the Garden and that Adam and Eve, meaning you and I, or both a man or a woman, can call upon Him anytime they need to speak with Him. We know that no secrets exist between them. We know that they are cared for and that all they require for survival is provided for them. No worries. We also know that they have a loving and open communication with the Lord. They just have to call out His name and He will be there. It's a wonderful, loving relationship.”

"But Sandra, we all know that when you die you go to Heaven. Not before. You are going to have a tough time trying to convince everyone otherwise. Particularly because that is what we have been lead to believe all of our lives."

"You are so right Oprah it is what we all have been led to believe. Now ask yourself, according to our Lord's Prayer, when will heaven be upon us?"

We both started to recite the prayer together.

"Our Father, who art in Heaven, hallowed be thy name.
Thy Kingdom come, Thy will be done on earth, as it is in Heaven." I butted in, "Thy Kingdom come, THY WILL BE DONE ON EARTH, as it is in Heaven! That's when, Oprah. Heaven on Earth is when God's knowings enters into us and we become ONE mind with Him."

"One with God." Oprah repeated after me in a tone that urged me to continue on.

"That is what I am saying to you that by discovering the Garden I have now discovered Heaven. Right here, on earth. And guess what else? God lives here!!!!!!! Right here in my Garden! I KNOW HIM! I speak to Him and He comes to me and He talks with me and He guides me! It is absolutely miraculous!!!"

"Now hold up there Sandra, why you? Why has God chosen you to talk to? Why are you so different from anyone else that claims they can talk to God? Why should I even believe what it is that you are telling me?"

At this moment in time, I took in a big breath and held back my truth. What I wanted to answer was "Cause I learned it and Oh yeah, did I forget to mention that I'm Eve, Oprah??? And cause I'm an angel!! God has placed into me this knowledge and I would share it with you right now if I thought for one moment you wouldn't high tail if out of here. That's how I know!"

But I did not let those private thoughts come out past my lips. After all, she just got here and I am not going to spring stuff like this on her so early in the day. Want to keep her butt in that chair a little longer than an hour. So, how am I gonna answer that? Think Sand, think! Keep the angel and Eve stuff out of it or you'll loose all credibility. Then I heard myself say.

"Oprah, we all can talk with God. WE ALL have the ability to be at home in The Garden with God, right now!" (Whew! Such a good truth!) I then said, "And Oprah, when you begin to align your will with the will of God, by acceptance of all that is, (including accepting pushy producers or meddling mothers-in-law) you relax with the control and the fixing and begin to see exactly what is."

"And from there into acceptance and then into peace?" Oprah offered up.

"Yeah. Just let go and let God. What else are you gonna do? Keep on fighting? Oprah, the only real battle that is happening on a day to day basis, the only real war that we gotta win, is the one in our heads!" And I pointed a finger at my head and tapped it a few times for emphasis.

"It's the battle for peace of mind! The battle to calm our perceived fears and that incessant voice that talks to us non-stop throughout the day. Sometimes I just want it to shut up!"

"Me too!

I know what you're talking about Sandra and it's hard to stop it."

"Damn hard Oprah, damn hard. So, accept that it will never shut up and then move into the knowing that you have the control over it. Now you're the pilot of your destiny once again and the fuel that you use to power your craft is positive thoughts."

“And that Ho’oponopono stuff you just talked about.”

“Yeah, that helps too. It helps a lot.”

“So, I think I understand a little bit more about what you’re saying Sandra.”

“Good. Oprah, I know God to be so good to us. He has a plan in all this, even though we cannot see the wisdom at this time. Trust in it.”

I then began to take in a deep breath and move my head slowly from side to side. Thinking of the feeling I get when I am talking with God, I was soon in that place where the two of us now were connected once again.

“Oprah, Oprah, Oprah, it' just such a great feeling that I, well, I just never want to leave Him. I never want to say good-bye to Him because being in His presence is so euphoric. So calming and peaceful. Everything just melts away. It's like being high. High on being with God.”

Oprah looked like she was searching for a way to respond to this. So, I offered up this.

“Oprah, I know that it sounds preachy to the ears of people who have yet to know God as intimately as I am claiming to have known Him. It’s the old adage, ‘If you only knew what I know’. But knowing God in your heart and in your being is much different that thinking about God, or reading His words. It is about” I paused, searching for the words.

“It’s like…”

And here I was stammering and searching wildly for an appropriate comparison. Then I heard myself blurting out. “It’s like having sex with God. It’s the ultimate intimacy.”

Now, I really saw Oprah's eyes light up with that one! So, I was quick to jump in with.

"I don't know if you ever had a crush on someone when you were a young girl Oprah?"

"A few" Oprah took her time answering this cause I think I stunned her with that last comment!

I jumped in with "Well, I had a serious crush on Kirk Douglas, Paul McCartney and a boy in grade five named Michael Meadly. It feels like a combination of that child-like infatuation and desire for something you are too young to understand and the adult realization of that fantasy. It involves all your being, all your senses. You now know God, as well as you know yourself."

"Sandra, are you telling me that you're 'Hot' for God?"

O.K., maybe I deserved that comment. I pressed my lips together and took in a deep breath. You know, many a hymn has been written that also has had the author of the hymn singing a love song to God. I just wish I could remember a friggin title to one right now when I really needed it!

"O.K., Oprah." I found myself saying out loud now.

"Knowing God is like having a love affair with Him. The same physical sensations that we have in a relationship are also present in the relationship that we share with God's spirit. It's euphoric. It is just that beautiful."

Preachy, I am being preachy. That's what I felt based on the reaction from Oprah. Silence. I'll leave it for now, I thought to myself.

With that I jumped up and offered Oprah some more lemonade.

"Would you care for another glass?"

Oprah reached for hers and handed it up to me. I kept on with my explanation as I headed towards the cottage door.

"Oprah, have you ever been touched by a Lama - you know, a Tibetan Lama?"

"No, I can't say that I have."

"Well, I have and the feeling that I had from it was nothing short of euphoria. Man, I was like high for two or three days. I didn't want to come back to earth but I was a Mom with three kids at the time and couldn't be floating around all day! Oprah, it's so awesome when God enters into you!"

Oprah smiled politely.

"Anyway, why don't you just sit tight and I'll be back in a second with the drinks."

I made my way into the cottage and opened the refrigerator where the lemonade was.

I muttered out loud to myself in a chastising tone, "Shit Sand… It's like having sex with God, Oprah?" I made a face and just shook my head from side to side. What a loser I am! I won't be surprised for one moment if when I get back out there she's on her cell speed dialing for the nearest cab to come and pick her up out of the rabbit hole!" Another heavy sigh from me as I grabbed two glasses and placed them on a tray. "Oh well, I am doing my best to describe it for her. Maybe she gets it? Sand, get a grip. It's going great now get out there and show her what you've got!" I smiled as I was very glad my Self finally decided to show up and shut down my ego!

“Accept what is cause it was meant to happen” I told myself over and over again as I carried the tray to the door and outside again where Oprah, surprisingly enough, was still there! Regaining my composure once again I carried out her lemonade in a stately fashion. Handed it to her and resumed my position sitting opposite her majesty.

Chapter Four

"Oprah I am so glad that you came here because I just love to be questioned. It makes it so much easier for me to let out what it is that I have been keeping inside myself for all these years."

We sat back down and settled in for what was going to be quite a story.

"Oprah, would you like me to share with you the time in my life when I was visited by an angel?"

Her eyes widened and she answered immediately to the affirmative. "Yes, Sandra, I would love to hear about that!"

Oprah still seemed interested.

Hmmm. I said to myself. Maybe what I had just shared with her wasn't so bad after all. I can be so hard on myself! I got up and took a moment to collect myself and bring back the feeling of the memory. I stared out at the trees and then turned to her and said,
"When I was a little girl Oprah, I remember one sunny spring morning."

I spoke slowly, and did my best to remember every little detail.
"I believe I was about four and a half at the time. It was a Sunday morning, quite early. I would guess around 7:00 or 7:30." I turned to face Oprah and gestured with a smile. "I used to get up very early when I was young to watch cartoons."

Oprah lit right up. "Oh yeah Sandra, me too!"

I smiled at her and responded "Which ones did you watch?"
"I'm trying to remember." She looked as if she was trying very hard to do just that. I rescued her with "I remember the first show that aired on Saturday mornings. It was called Diver Dan." I

began to giggle.

"Is that the one with Baron Barracuda?"

"Yes. I believe that it was!"

"Honestly Oprah, it was great." We both giggled at the same memory and I soon resumed my story.

"Anyway, that particular morning, I got up and instead of just going downstairs in my pajamas and watching cartoons, I began to get myself dressed. Now remember Oprah, I was only four and a half years of age at the time. I most likely was just learning to dress myself because I can recall how hard I had to concentrate in order to correctly put on what was appropriate for me to wear."

"Seriously Sandra, you can remember that far back?"

"Like it was yesterday. Anyways, when I look back upon this, I don't know why I would have chosen to do this."

"Unless you were lead to do it."

"Exactly. I must have been because after I got dressed, I went straight outside. I believe I wanted to test myself on how far from home I could go without getting lost. I made a deal with myself that I would venture out and as soon as I didn't know the people who were living in the houses I was passing, I would turn around and go home."

"Sandra, you sound like such a smart girl, even at four!"

I nodded in agreement and then continued on. "Smart and an adventurer even at the tender age of four!" and I smiled and continued.

"I believe I got as far as Christine Lacey's house and then I didn't know any more people after that, so I turned around and began to head back home."

Oprah's eyes were as big as saucers as I was explaining my explorations. She couldn't help herself cause she spit out, "What on earth child! A little four year old out on the street alone at 7:30 in the morning? Why I am breaking out into a sweat just thinking about the possible ramifications of such an action!"

"Me too Oprah, me too. You certainly would rush into the fear nowadays if a child that young was out on the street, unattended."

"Yeah, like you'd have to answer to Children's Aid or something like that!"

"Well, back then, it was not like that. When I think about it Oprah, it was a time when fear didn't dictate our actions. People lived in trust. Fear never really entered into it."

"I guess so" Oprah scratched her chin and in the silence that ensued, she pondered for a moment what I had just said.

"Sandra, I can remember now that we are sharing, I can remember times in my own childhood as well when that fear that we were just talking about was not around. Kids playing on the streets with one another. Out all day bike riding, laughing and playing with one another."

"Having adventures!"

"Yes, having grand adventures."

"It's changed somewhat."

"Yes, it has. It's changed quiet a lot hasn't it?" Then we both grew quiet once more.

I continued to retell the story, ever so slowly. “Anyways, I turned towards Home, and I began to notice that there was absolutely no one around. And Oprah, I mean no one. Not even a squirrel, scampering across the street. Or a bird, chirping in a tree. It was dead silent. I was singing to myself as I was running up and down through the ditches along the side of the road. I can remember as well, thinking that the grass was not yet green, and that I should have thought to put a coat on because the air was chilly.

I paused and smiled at the memory.

“Then I remembered looking up. I began to observe the scene ahead of me. Oprah, I can see it all so clearly, even now. There was no movement. None at all. The atmosphere had become very still. It was as if someone had taken a vacuum and sucked up all the air. I noticed then, that there also was no sound. No sounds what so ever. I was thinking to myself how strange this was when all of a sudden, this warmth came up behind me and Oprah, the only way to describe it to you is that this wonderful feeling came over me.” And here I stood up to demonstrate.

“And remember Oprah, this all took place in a matter of seconds. Only it felt, as if I was moving in slow motion. And this presence, why it felt familiar. It felt comforting and assuring. And warm! Oh, and Oprah, I wasn’t the least bit afraid. Then, I heard a voice in my right ear and the voice simply said to me,
“You know that you are not alone.” and I smiled to myself with the knowing of it and responded to the presence in my mind,
“I know.” And then this warmth covered me all over from head to toe and I felt happy Oprah. I felt so loved, so watched over and yes, I was full of the knowing that I was indeed, not alone.

We both stared at each other in that moment, Oprah and I. I took my time here so that we both could allow in what I had just told her. Tears were welling up in both our eyes.

“I believe I was visited by one of God’s angels, Oprah.”

“I believe that you were too Sandra.”

“Would you like a Kleenex?”

“Yes, please. If it is not too much trouble.”

I went inside of the cottage. Grabbed a box that was located on the little table by the television and quickly headed back out doors. I passed the box to Oprah. She took a tissue and I grabbed one for myself. A moment later, dry eyes achieved once more, I continued on with my story.

“Oprah that was the angel Gabrielle sent by God to tell me that I was being watched over.”

“You’re telling me that at four years of age Sandra, you knew that God's angel had come to you?” Oprah smiled.

“It's not that I knew what it was at that time, Oprah. You see as a child, I didn’t know that this was even an out of the ordinary occurrence! As far as I knew, it happened to everybody. I just kept it to myself. It was not until I began recollecting my childhood that I even gave it much relevance.”

“But you do now.”

"Oh yeah, now I know that it's a pretty big deal to have that happen to you.”

Oprah asked me, “Sandra, how did you know that it was real?”

“Good question Oprah.” I paused and then answered.

“Well, I was awake for one thing. And secondly I was alone. I believe that God can come to you when you are alone. Plus, the stillness of everything around me. Now that was freaky.”

"I bet it was."

"Oprah, until you experience a visit from an angel, or the Holy Spirit, well, it's really hard to explain it."

"I think that you're doing a great job Sandra. I have had many Ah-ah moments, but nothing like what you're telling me."

I paused for a moment. I then said to her, "Really? Think back to your own childhood, Oprah. I believe there was a time when you were in a sandbox playing all by yourself. It was there I believe that you began to speak with your angels."

There was a very long pause as I had given Oprah time to think. Then the look upon Oprah's face changed and you could tell by her expression, she had remembered exactly what I was talking about!

"How did you know about that?"

"Gee Oprah," I teased, "I must be psychic or something?"

"Very funny." She exclaimed.

I smiled at her and then said, "I had another angel visit me in 2009, but that was not the same as this. Also, in 1981 when my father was ill I remember calling into me God's strength, His Holy Spirit, to deal with the situation and sure enough, this energy came into me only this time, it stayed in me for quite awhile."

"So, what's the difference between a visit from an angel and that of The Holy Spirit?"

"Good question. My personal answer for that is, an angel comes, delivers the message that it has been entrusted with and then goes. The Holy Spirit on the other hand, enters into you and stays for awhile."

"How long? How long does it stay for Sandra?" Oprah was keen to hear the answer.

"Until its presence is no longer needed in you. It could be a matter of days, weeks or longer. It all depends on what God's plan for you is."

"Or how long you're needing back-up!" We both smiled at each other and I said, "Exactly right! Oprah, when I was four, having that angel come to me and tell me that I was not alone, well, it was one of the most beautiful moments of my life because I felt so safe and under God's care. It was God's way of letting me know that He is always with me, even when I am not aware of it."

"So did you tell anyone about this happening after you remembered it?"

"Maybe a few, but it had more to do with me seeing that event in my life as an important puzzle piece when I was seeking out who I was. You see Oprah, when you look back over your life you will remember certain events, both positive and negative. Take those memories and begin to assemble a picture of who it is that you are by where it is that you have been and what you have experienced. Put the pieces together and you can begin to actually see who it is that you are."

"Puzzle pieces!" She exclaimed. "I have heard of puzzle pieces before Sandra."

"Most of us have by now. Taking note of important events and memories that had taken place in your life. Things that I had accomplished, lessons that I had learned, people that I had met. I began to see a pattern emerge that had to do a lot with God."

"Such as......"

"Such as how it was that I discovered who Jesus was through my Auntie Marion."

"Your Aunt Marion?" Oprah looked at me in a way that asked. "Tell me about Auntie Marion?"

Chapter Five

“My favorite Aunt. She was my Mom's sister and she lived in Kitchener/Waterloo, Ontario. I was visiting her house once and she was teaching Sunday school at the time. My own parents were not church goers and I had no memories of attending church before then. So, she took me with her one Sunday morning. I had such a wonderful peaceful feeling inside of me after finding out who Jesus was. I loved sitting with the other children and coloring in pictures of Jesus and the praying hands.”

“The praying hands?” she asked.

“The famous hands held together, holding the rosary, praying?”

Silence from Oprah as she gave me a look of not knowing and then immediately brightened up as the picture came into her mind.

“Yes, yes, I know the ones.”

“Right, well those hands became a puzzle piece in my life representing the presence of God. When my own son Mike first attended Sunday school he created a card similar to the one that I had myself created. Oprah, it contained that same set of praying hands.”

“The exact same picture of praying hands was on your son's card? Had he ever seen the card that you made as a child, Sandra?”

“No, it was long gone.”

“Then how did he know to do that?”

“That's my point. He couldn't have. It was a sign” I surmised.

“Oprah, to further the story, I usually keep all my children’s wonderful creations from school and Sunday school in a box that I store in the basement.” Oprah nodded as I continued. “So, I stored the card he made as a child in that box. Time goes on to some ten years later and my son grows up and becomes a teenager. Like most guys wanting to be cool, he goes out after receiving his first government income tax check back, and he couldn't wait to go out and get a tattoo.”

“You let your teenage son go out and get a tattoo?” Oprah somewhat chastised.

“Well, he knew I would not approve. Of course he did his best to hide it from me. Eventually it comes out. When it did, he proudly rolled up his sleeve to reveal a set of praying hands!”

“I knew you couldn't get mad at me Mom if I got something that you'd like!”

Appreciating the sentiment, but not the tattoo... I just shook my head. About a month later, I was downstairs and I saw the box where I kept my children's old cards and drawings. Was I ever surprised to see that card that had to have been ten years old supporting a sticker with those same praying hands! It must have been meant to be!”

“You’re telling me that your son getting a tattoo of a set of praying hands has meaning?”

“Yes, for me as well as for Him.”

“How so, Sandra?”

“Well, that puzzle piece tied in not only with my past, but my son's as well. It really gave me a clue that somehow my son was also tied into God and the Jesus story. Oprah, I found out that during the time of Christ, My son Michael was none other than

King Herod! My other son that you met, Doug. He was Pilot."

"How do you know that, Sandra?" she asked, astounded that I could say such a thing with such certainty.

"Oprah, God has given me the gift of knowing who people were in past lifetimes." I continued. There was a pause between us.

"You see Oprah, along this journey towards God, if you stick to it and you are persistent, God will reward you."

"How does He reward you?" she asked.

"He gives you gifts along the way. One of the gifts he has given me is the ability to know who people were in past lifetimes. Somehow, I just seem to attract to me people that happened to have walked the earth at the time of Christ."

"Really?" Oprah was somewhat dumbfounded.

"Oprah, our spirits have been around forever. We are the all that is. In other words, we are all connected. We keep on running into ourselves and our previous lifetimes."

"What does that mean?"

"It means that from what I have learned over the years is that we continually are connecting with our past in our present. How we handle the release of past hurts allows us to be in the present which in turn lays the foundation for our future."

"But isn't the present where all the power is and shouldn't you strive to be in that place" Oprah somewhat demanded from me.

"Well, yes. The power of being in the now is you can connect to the 'all that is'. You and Eckhart Tolle have recently planted that wonderful seed in us all! Well done!"

Oprah smiled broadly with that compliment.

"I am able to connect into the now of someone's spirit and I can feel from them where it is that they have been. I also can tell which life time they are most needing to discover or hear about and why."

"Really?" Oprah was fascinated. So I continued on.

"And Oprah, most of our spirits have all been here for a very long time." I paused and then added, "Some spirits however are new to us; some are here from different places all together."

"What are you saying? That some spirits have not always been on the earth?"

"That's right. I have met some alien spirits that are here from other places. Some are on their first trip to us. We refer to them as 'New Souls'. On the other hand some souls have been with us for the better part of our existence upon this planet."

"So, I am interested in how you know this" Oprah asked.

"Well, I have talked to a lot of peoples' spirits. Oprah, I don't judge them, I just accept them. Honestly, if you want to know the truth, some people's spirits, that are not from the earth plane can have a pretty tough time adjusting to life on earth."

"Really?"

"Most are walking around among us with the feeling inside of them that they do not belong here. It's a lonely feeling. They too have to figure out who they are and know that they are also on another mission and that mission is to be of great service in this transitional time."

I then laughed, "I can remember this one fellow I met at a party who was messed up."

Oprah responded, "Really?"

"Oprah, this guy was so socially out of place."

"How do you mean?"

"He was rude, obnoxious. Never did he say the right things. Always he ended up offending people. Finally, at one point in the evening, I sat down and told him why he was so messed up. Do you know what he did when I told him the reason he was having so many problems was because his spirit was alien to this earth plane and it was his first time here?"

"No, what did he do?" Oprah was wide-eyed.

"He sat and just cried with relief."

"I knew I was different" he cried to me. "I knew that I didn't fit in here."

"Oprah, do you know that this man, like other alien spirits here, can fall into despair because they feel alone and not like others? They may begin drinking or acting out in a self hurting manner because they are feeling so sorry for themselves Many become loners. Once these people identify that they have special powers of healing and other gifts that can be given, they will be able to contribute in a powerful way."

"How powerful, Sandra."

Oprah was into what I was telling her.

"Oprah, some are great doctors, social workers. Even comedians"
"Comedians, why would you center them out?" Oprah kind of laughed at this.

"Because there is great healing power in laughter. Good comedians are spiritual doctors in disguise. Probably some of the most intelligent beings among us. Oprah, it takes an intelligent mind to remain present and see with such clarity the obvious in people. There may be many people trying to be funny. However, the truly gifted, they rise to the top. Oprah, there are so many things that are happening that are soooo beyond what we consider as 'Normal'. You best just keep an open mind and let go of all negative judgments."

"Well, amen to that, my friend. Amen to that!"

"I only hope I can stress enough to those people who may end up reading this book that these individuals, visitors from other dimensions, are indeed strong warriors for the greater good, who, Oprah, can begin to help us turn our planet around."

Oprah looked side to side. "So you don't feel that it is a bit too far fetched this idea that there are other soul, spirits from out there?"

"Not really Oprah. I think that there are people who have already accepted their, let's call it uniqueness. I think that these spirits are in clubs all over the world helping to support one another."

"Such as?"

"Such as Star War Clubs."

"What do you think of Scientology?"

"I have yet to really learn about it. However, I could hazard a guess that some of their theories are along those lines. I still have not educated myself in that."

"I have a few good friends that are into it."

“Mmmmm, now who would that be?" I smiled and so did she.

Chapter Six

"Oprah, getting back to my ability for reading past lives and spirits. I find that most people, if you listen to them, hear what they are saying and how they are saying it to you, they will eventually tell you who it is that they have been. If you listen objectively to what terminologies that they are using, what stories they are telling, you can get a pretty good sense of who it is that they were in the past. By that I mean, I can get a sense of what it is that they need to know about themselves and my hope is that when I give them that knowledge, state it out loud, that they now have a chance to integrate that information and work with it to see if they can make sense of it." I paused.

"You know. See if their past life is showing itself through clues in our present life."

"I see." Oprah responded, then commented…

"So you have made known from this book, that I am Moses in a past lifetime."

"Yes. I know that you have had other lifetimes as well Oprah. However, this is the lifetime that you are to come into awareness of at this time. It is through your knowing of this Oprah, and your acceptance of this, that you can prepare yourself for the knowledge of another lifetime that will help to carry you forward."

"So you're telling me is that my lifetime as Moses is what I am to focus on now and that when I need to know about other past lifetimes of mine, they will be made known to me?"

"Well, when it's time for you to know, then they will be revealed to you."

“So what you’re saying is that you DO know, about another past lifetime of mine and you’re just not telling me?”

I smiled and informed her, “The information will be given when your conscious mind is ready. Not until. For now, just learn all it is that you can about Moses and his life. What he accomplished. Keep bringing it back to your own life and search for similarities.”

“Oh.” Oprah stopped there and took a good, long drink of lemonade. I could see that she was assimilating much of the information that she had just received. Either that or sulking.

“It's about making connections. Michael's choice of tattoo alerted me to the possibility of a connection. Oprah, once you operate by the code that nothing happens by accident you begin to live the life of a sleuth. A detective. You begin to search for the hidden meanings behind people and circumstances.”

“Yes Sandra, I already know this.”

“Did you read The Celestine Prophecy?”

“I did back in the nineties. That was an amazing book, was it not?”

“Oh, man that book was one of the main reasons I was able to handle the spirit of God when it came into me in 1994! But I am getting ahead of myself. Oprah, my son Michael walked the earth as King Herod over 2000 years ago!”

“But Sandra, it just blows me away that you can be so sure.”

“Oprah, I know this because I KNOW it.”

“You'll have to do better than that Sandra. Explain, please.”

“Perhaps the best gift that I have received on my journey towards knowing God is the gift of knowing. Oprah, it's amazing. It's a feeling that comes when the truth is made known to me. I can experience it when I ask a question of God and He puts the knowing into me. I don't even have to ask or to speak to receive it. It's as if the truth is being revealed to me and I just KNOW it to be true. Like you know that Gayle is your best friend. You know that you are SUCH an important person in this world.”

I paused… “Or maybe you just don't yet how important that you REALLY are Oprah” I said under my breath, then continued… “Oprah, you know your favorite food. What you like to drink. A favorite movie or book. You just know. So, now imagine that when you are having a conversation with someone and either one of you gets in touch with the world of spirit and something profound is then shared between you. Well, it’s like a truth is spoken and when this truth that is spoken is a universal truth and has meaning, a strange thing occurs. You will both begin to get goose bumps.”

I was demonstrating to Oprah now on my arm as I continued to explain.

“It’s as if your DNA is reacting to what is being said and you both break out in these goose bumps at the same time.”

“Sandra, I have felt this before. It’s like a wonderment. Some inexplicable thing and yes you’re right, it occurs when I am sharing my spirit self with someone.”

“It’s so cool isn’t it Oprah?”

“Why, yes it is. But you know what, until now I really didn’t know how to explain it.”

“Well it happens a lot to me. Most often, when I am sharing with someone who it was that their spirit once walked the earth as.”

“It’s kind of a validation isn’t it, Sandra?”

“Yes Oprah, that’s exactly what it is: validation that what you have just shared is true. Not just your truth, but a universal truth.”

“Meaning it’s a truth for us all?”

“Yes, that is exactly what I mean. Oprah, this is so great that you know this!”

“And Sandra, it is so strange that we are talking about this now because I have been noticing that it is happening a lot more now.”

“And it will begin to happen more and more Oprah as we approach the 2012 mark.”

“Why is that Sandra?”

“Because the world of spirit is beginning to make itself known now.”

“And that is pretty much why we are all experiencing this push towards knowing ourselves and our purpose in being here”

“Right on! You hit the nail on the head!”

“Oprah, the more information that we know about ourselves in this lifetime, the more information we are given from our past lifetimes. In other words, if you take on the task of knowing yourself and all there is to know about you from now, back to your childhood, then you are able to release past painful experiences. In doing that, you are giving the emotion voice and expression. You free yourself up to learn more about yourself, more than just, this life.”

“Really?”

"Well, I was telling you to gather up the clues of your life and try to see if there is a pattern to it. My pattern seemed to lead me towards God. Remember Oprah, I was telling you how I had been introduced to Jesus through my aunt and others."

"Yes."

"Well, I used to get to go to church with my neighbors. It always made me shake my head how God was calling me to know Him and he used my family and neighbors to do it!"

"How old were you when this started?" she asked.

"Well, I guess it would have been six or seven years of age."

"Really? You were keen to go to church at that young age?"

"Most definitely. Having that experience with my Aunt made me want to know more. I was able to go occasionally but did not get much education until I was about fourteen when I attended confirmation classes."

"What denomination were you confirmed under?" Oprah queried. "Anglican. I was married in an Anglican church as well but did not attend regularly until I began having a family. Then, I switched over to the United Church."

"Why the United Church?"

"Because my husband was confirmed United. And you may be well aware that if you can get them to go to church with you Oprah, you'll make the necessary sacrifices!"

"Got it Sandra." We both had a little smile at that one!

"So, it had been awhile by then since I had attended church and I found that I was almost spiritually dead inside."

"Why was that?" Oprah asked.

"I think it had to do with the fact that I had let that part of my life go for such awhile. That connection with God. I thought that I had it all figured out. I felt that I didn't need God. I figured that I knew just about everything that there was to know. I was a control freak. In truth Oprah, I lived in fear. I was so busy trying to control my environment and everyone in it in order to make myself safe, that I lost track of the magic of bringing in the new."

"Bringing in the new, means?"

"Watching and allowing. Being a passenger upon occasion instead of the driver. I found that this helps you to let go and just become the observer. If you can manage to just watch, without judgment you enter into a new way of being. Your friend Eckhart Tolle was big into that."

"Yes, I learned so much doing that series with him. It sounds like you enjoyed the series as well?"

"Oprah, I read the book, watched all the lessons and joined in some classes. I even began to start my own group! It has been a Godsend to me, Oprah. To the world. How courageous for you to come forward with that!" I then began to laugh and then said out loud but to myself, "Considering who it is that YOU are I mean."

Oprah, who never misses a beat was quick to pick that up and responded, "Oh yeah, about that Moses thing." Oprah squinted and looked at me. She then added, "Is that who I really am? Who it is that I was I mean? Sandra, tell me."

I just stopped and stared at her and for the first time I really gave her all my intuitive attention. I became in tune with her true essence. Silence followed as I took in numerous deep breaths and became very still.

"Oprah, why else do you think that God has placed you in the position that He has? You leading His people into a new way of 'Being' on our earth?"

Silence followed. Oprah sat back in her chair and I in mine and we both just drank in the moment. We sat together for a minute or two; just the two of us being in the moment. It was incredibly powerful for both.

"You know Oprah, actually finishing 'The Day That Oprah Came To Visit My Garden' was quite difficult for me."

"Why was that Sandra?"

"The truth is… and here I paused for another reflective moment, and then confessed to her, "I have been afraid."

"Afraid, Sandra? You were actually afraid?"

"Honestly, I was. Oprah, my work for the past twenty some odd years, has been to write and journal God's word as He gives it to me. Quite frankly, some things are so controversial that I honestly believed if I were to publish it, well…"

Oprah leaned over and placed her hand upon mine, looked into my eyes and asked me straight-up, "Sandra, what is it that you have found out that could have made you so afraid to come forward with? What is it that God has revealed to you that you were so afraid to share?"

I looked down and pulled my hand away.

"What God tells me and what He reveals to me. You talk about your occasional 'Aha' moments. Oprah, that is pretty much all I get when God talks with me. It's like being on constant Aha!"

"But what was so frightening?" she paused and reached over and put her hand on my arm.

“Were you afraid that no one would believe you?”

“Yes that, and the information that I was channeling from God was pretty significant.”

“Such as....” Oprah was leading me on.

“Such as, He wants us to know that He is opening up the Gates.”

“The Gates?”

“Yes.”

“Thee gates.”

“Yes.”

“Thee gates as in the Gates of Heaven.”

“Yup. The gates that when opened will lead you back home to God. The gates that allow the barrier between heaven and earth to be lifted. In other words, Oprah, the two worlds will eventually be as one.”

“Heaven and earth shall be as one?”

“God will begin to reveal himself to His children.”

“What do you mean?”

“Well, God is telling me that He is beginning to place more of Himself inside of His children. Then I am assuming that His children will be the ones beginning to awaken. To awaken as to what is actually going on around us in this present time.”

Oprah took that information in and was quiet. I was also quiet. Both of us were allowing this to percolate. Allowing also for the universe to either send her another question or me another piece of information.

Oprah won.

"So, what you are saying is that if you are not beginning to awaken, then you may not be a child of God?"

"What I am saying is that if you are not beginning to awaken, then you'd better begin to ask yourself why? Oprah, we are all called to God in His time, not ours. If you have not been called to awaken at this time, it does not mean that you will not be. It may however, indicate to you that you are perhaps not being plugged into the present."

"What does being in the present have to do with it Sandra?"

"Well, God could be calling you at this very minute to begin your journey home towards Him and you aren't aware of it cause it's a subtle calling."

"You mean He is coming to you in little ways."

"Exactly. Oprah, you have heard of the two by four theory?"

"Nope."

"Well, it states that your lessons come to you softly at first, like a feather on your cheek. If you don't pay attention, the next thing is you get a hit from a stick on the leg."

"Meaning the universe is wishing to wake you up to something and now it's going to move in a way to get your attention somewhat more aggressively."

"Right. And if you still do not listen or pay attention to what is going on in your life?"

And here I stood up and mimicked a baseball player standing at the plate and as I swung through at the ball I shouted "BAM" Right in the face."

"There ain't no mistaken that message!"

"Right you are Oprah. Right you are!" The two by four theory is widely used by God and His angels to get one of God's children who is off on the wrong track, back on the road to the straight and narrow."

We both had a chuckle at this.

"You know Oprah, coming home to God can just be as simple as asking Him to take you there."

"What about a confession? I thought that was mandatory?"

"Ask Him to take you home. Ask Him to forgive you your sins. Tell Him that you believe in His Son. Those three things for me are like a launch code."

"Launch code?" Oprah raised her brow.

"Yeah, from all of my writing over the past twenty some odd years, it appears that those three things when spoken to God, begin a process."

"A process?"

"When you ask God to forgive you your sins, acknowledge that Christ is our Savior and then ask God to take you Home, you're pretty much in the Kingdom of Heaven. Like saying those three things launch you into a life with Christ as your Savoir. Your keeper. It means he's got your back from now on and you never have to worry."

"Oh, but Sandra, people love to worry. It's like an addiction for many."

"You have that right Oprah! I think faith is a tough thing to live by. You really have to be present to your relationship with God. To the point that anything that arises in your life, your day to day existence, you have to continually tell yourself that God is watching over you. Not to worry, have faith. Do you agree Oprah?"

"Well yeah. It is hard though Sandra. I often catch myself thinking that I have to do it all myself."

"Me too, Oprah!" It is a constant thing right now, having to remind myself that as children of God, there is absolutely no need for me to worry."

"Do you worry about much Sandra?" Oprah asked.

"I guess if I do worry, I worry about getting it down right. Getting down God's meaning in this book I wrote for you Oprah. For you and everyone else. I worry about all God's children finding their way Home. Home to God. So, that is why I wrote this book. To put in my contribution to the world. I have a gift. I seem to be able to speak with God and it is because of this gift that I wish to share what it is that I receive when I speak with Him."

"So, God telling you that the Gates of Heaven are now opening…" Oprah was leading me into an answer.

"It's my purpose to tell His children not to be afraid of this time, but to welcome it. So much fear is being raised and there is no need for it. I am hoping to shift our collective consciousness away from fear and onto what is really happening out there!"

"Which is…?"

"The gates of Heaven are opening up and the degree to which you are connected with yourself, the present and with God is the measure of how this experience will pan out for you."

"Wow. O.K. Sandra. O.K." Oprah just sat back and had a bit of a breather. We both just paused and looked down, gathering our thoughts.

"I'm gonna recap what it is that I think that you are trying to tell us. I hear you telling me that God is lifting up the barrier between Heaven and Earth. That what we all refer to as the pearly gates is actually a barrier in the mind?"

"It is the veil that when lifted brings us into the knowingness of God. We become one with Him and with one another. But it is more than just words Oprah. It is the actual experience of living on earth in that connectedness. We begin to be in Heaven, right here, right now."

"Got it Sandra. Got it." Oprah paused. I did too and then went on with my next thought.

Chapter Seven

"Right now, it's about being in the moment and being in a state of higher energy. Keeping yourself in a positive state of mind and being love. Being loving ensures you this energy. Higher vibrations occur when you are in a state of love, Oprah, not fear. If you are in a state of love, then your energy is lifted. You are functioning on a higher vibration. This lifts you up! It lifts us all up. Oprah do you want to know one of my favorite comparisons that I like to use is?"

"Yeah."

"I always laugh to myself, when I think about people who say that they are not into the 'New Age' stuff. Imagine Oprah, if you were living in Europe during the birth of The Renaissance, and you were proclaiming that you were not a 'Renaissance Man or Woman'. That you didn't believe in it. It would be going on around you regardless of whether you were 'into it' or not. That is what is happening with our world and on your television show Oprah! Weather people are watching it or not, the shift you are facilitating is still happening. Heck Oprah, New Age is exactly what is says it is. A NEW TIME. A NEW WAY OF BEING. A NEW WAY TO THINK. So, if it is happening to most of us, this new way of being, then it will eventually happen to us all. We will all be in it because the majority of people will be co-creating it!"

"You know what Sandra?" Oprah said this as a statement, more than a question.

I nodded at her to continue on.

"I heard that's how Christ came to be with us here on the earth. That at the time, the people of Israel were collectively praying for a Messiah to help them break free of the tyranny they were under.

That so many people were praying for the same thing that they ended up creating the coming of Jesus."

"Hey, you know what Oprah, I heard that from my Biblical Professor as well. The same story."

"Yup, and do you know what else Sandra?"

"What Oprah?"

"I think the same thing is within our grasp again, only we have yet to realize it."

"I agree whole-heartedly with you, my friend. More than you know." And here I paused and smiled to myself. Then I continued…"It's about getting as many people as possible to stand up and claim their creator power."

"But what about those people who are not in a co-creating place – a place of fear?"

"It is those people who are not strong in God and love that are channels for that fear. Using fear as a motivator is what the lower vibration forces, are all about. If those who would choose to control us can manage to place God's children in a constant state of fear, then what would be our chances to create a positive outcome?"

"So what I hear you telling me Sandra is that if enough people can raise their vibrations through love and positive thinking, that we can collectively create something as beautiful as heaven on earth?"

"Or the second coming of Christ" I added, just to get her to think about it.

Oprah paused for a second, but did not give that last statement much thought and then proceeded with, “However, if we give into fear and allow our vibrations to fall, than we cannot create our Heaven on earth because our power decreases through fear?”

“Yup. That is exactly what I am saying.”

“Oprah, what you are leading with this show is a cultural revolution. We will all begin to use the new language when speaking to one another. The more people who begin to speak and think as if we are having a ‘New Earth’, or ‘A New Heaven on Earth’, then that’s what we will create.”

“Now that is cool” Oprah smiled.

“Oprah, it was after all, Moses who lead his people into a new land. Think about it. That is exactly what you, Oprah, are also doing in your time, only the actual physical land, has already BEEN discovered, it’s the land of the spirit that you seek.”

Oprah gave me a puzzled look. I went on to explain.

“Oprah, you are leading people into a new earth. Get It? It’s still the same physical land, the earth itself has already been discovered – it’s not new. What you are doing differently is to lead your people into a new world of the spirit. In fact, this IS history repeating itself, only it’s going on now instead of thousands of years ago. And it’s not the physical land of Israel that you are seeking. It is the entrance into the ‘New Age’ of being one on all the land, with the spirit. The spirit of God.

“To simplify what you are telling me Sandra, would be to say that I am doing the Moses thing again. Same souls, just repeating the same story, over and over and over again until we get to where God is leading us.”

“Yesssssssss!” I was elated to have gotten my point across.

Chapter Eight

"Oprah, I just had a message from spirit come to me."

I paused while I began to receive a channeling from the 'All That Is'.

"Oprah, I am believing that those people among us who are beginning to awaken are truly the dead among us."

"What does that mean?"

"I'm not sure, just let me continue."

"Ooops - sorry." Oprah put a hand over her mouth and grimaced, apologizing under her breath. I smiled at her and continued to explain.

"In the Bible they tell us that the dead, the dead souls of those who have come before us will rise and be the first to awaken. So, if the people who are awakening now, are past dead souls, then I am telling you that the souls that have died in the past at the time when you were Moses, are coming forth first at this time. They are the ones reading the New Earth and watching your show!"

"O.K. let me clarify what it is that you are saying."

"Channeling."

"Right. Channeling. Sandra, you are saying that past dead souls of people who were alive at the same time I was alive being Moses...."

"Yeah..."

"Those are the souls that are currently reading A New Earth and that is who they once were? Moses' people?"

"Right. I am getting that those of us who are beginning to open up now are also the dead souls that were present when Jesus walked the earth as well."

"Go slowly please." Oprah insisted. Then she added under her breath, but loud enough so that I could still hear her.

"You might as well throw in Atlantis while you're at it." And she shuffled in her chair. But I did hear her and immediately throw in "Atlantis as well."

Now Oprah, somewhat agitated at all this information spoke up.

"How can you sit there and tell me that all dead souls from all those past times in history are now resurrecting themselves?"

"I am telling you because it is true, In fact all dead souls and knowledge of our souls past lifetimes here on this earth plane are now rising up!"

"Ghosts from the past, Sandra?"

"Ghost from the past and spirits dead and buried, Operahhhhh" I said with eyes wide open and head moving side to side.

"So, what?" she asked in a teasing manner.

"So, who ya gonna call?"

Then in a resounding response we both shouted out -- "Ghostbusters!" and had a good laugh.

"I needed a good laugh right around now Sandra."

I was so thrilled to be having fun and laughing with my guest.

"You see the thing that I have learned about being able to read and know past lives is that the past is also the present. What has once happened will re-enact itself again. This is the case with you. The energy that moved through you long ago as Moses, is now entering you once more as Oprah."

Oprah said nothing. She just stared at me.

"O.K. What I am saying is that those people whom were present when you were Moses are the people who will begin to open up to the ideas behind 'A New Earth' the fastest."

"Because" She managed to squeak out as she took another sip of her drink, "Because God's placing His energy inside of them once again. Their soul/spirits remember you. Oprah. Their spirits already know that you are Moses, not their conscious minds. When they read this information, they will consciously begin to remember."

"People will begin to remember I am Moses?"

"Yes. And this truth will send a vibration that is stored inside of their DNA and this release of truth will cause them to get those tingly goose bump things that we were talking about."

"O.K."

"People will believe that you are Moses. Their soul/spirits will resonate with the fact that they have followed you before and know deep inside themselves that you are to be trusted. When you were Moses, they witnessed the miracles that you once performed. Oprah, they will not doubt you because their spirits know you."

Pause, big breath in. I continued.

"It is the same energy that was present on earth when you were living as Moses. That same energy is now back again in this life time."

"For what purpose, Sandra?"

"Before, it was Moses leading his people out of slavery. I believe that is the case now as well. It's just not a physical slavery Oprah. It's a slavery of the mind."

"You mean we have been made slaves to our old ways of thinking."

"I couldn't have said it any better, Oprah. Exactly right."

"So God placing His energy in me and His people is preparing us for a journey."

"You got it! History is repeating itself once again! What was, is. And what is now, is forever."

"And this is so because??? Oprah?"

"Because God wills it so."

"Yes, because God wills it so. Oprah, I could not have dreamed up this information. It was revealed to me. So, I know enough from my conversations with God, that there is wisdom in it. I will just sit back until the wisdom is revealed to me."

And here I sat back and twiddled my thumbs and looked around the yard portraying someone just waiting around for something to happen.

Oprah leaned forward and asked.

"So, the wisdom for me is?"

"Just know and watch. Even without the awareness that your soul/spirit is Moses, you were already doing the work of Moses."

"Yeah, I guess that I was." Oprah was shaking her head up and down in an affirmative nod.

"So, just relax and let things come to you."

"O.K."

"But it's kind of neat now because you are able to have this knowledge in the back of your mind all the time now, just as a reminder that you too Oprah are not alone. God has got your back. Expect miracles!"

"Oh I have seen my fair share of miracles." And she stopped and looked over at me and I was just sitting there smiling at her. She smiled at me and I said to her.

"Well now Oprah. Is That Right?" We both began to giggle.

"O.K. smarty pants. I get it."

"You will now be validated sooo often with this truth Oprah. It will come up again and again for you. That is why I would encourage you to read about all that you can about Moses because it is the life time that you are closely mirroring now."

"Yes. Yes. I can see the wisdom in this."

"One more detail that I have left out about the dead souls rising."

"Oh yeah? And what detail would that be Sandra?"

"It would be the detail of about four or five years ago when my daughter and I were up here the summer that she had mono."

"Yeah. What happened?"

"Well, one day we were sitting out the front, and as we were talking, I saw the face of my dead father coming through Caitlyn's face."

"What do you mean you saw the face of your dead father coming through your daughters face?"

"I mean just what I said. The face of my daughter was no longer her own and I saw my father's face morphing through until I could see it so clearly, my daughter became my father."

"Really? How could that be Sandra?"

"I believe that it was the soul/spirit of my father showing himself to me through a face that I loved."

"To what end?"

"I believe that the souls of the dead rising means that the soul/spirits of all those that we have come to know as 'loved ones' from all of our lifetimes are now and will be making themselves known to us."

"So you're telling me that I just maybe looking at Gayle sometime and her face is gonna morph into somebody else's?"

"Yes. I have had it happen more than once where I could see the faces of numerous people come through one person. I knew by witnessing this that there is a phenomenon happening that is and will be occurring on a more frequent basis."

"Well, were you not frightened when you saw this happen?"

"No, I wasn't. But I think my daughter thought that I had just about lost it. I began to cry and reached out and said 'Oh Daddy I miss you so much.' And I began to cry and hug her as I would have hugged my father."

"Did you explain to her what you saw?"

"Oh yes, I did at the time and afterwards as well. I know she heard me but I think that she also must have thought it a bit strange."

"I know I would have been freaking out."

"It's actually the world of spirit allowing us to view its presence."

"I guess you're right. I don't know what to think about this Sandra. I mean, am I to understand that I will begin seeing other people's faces in the people around me?"

"Yes. Yes that is a possibility. It's because, like I said, the souls of our dead loved ones or even the souls of loved ones of past lives may come forward for you to see."

"And if this happens, don't panic."

"No, don't panic. Just become a witness to it. Perhaps they have a message for you or perhaps they just want you to be aware that they are there. It's a sign of the end of days Oprah. It is what we are told will happen and it is happening to many people."

"It is eh?"

"Oh yeah. Only because the visitation can be so brief. People doubt it. Oprah, why do you think that there are so many people now reporting spirit sightings?"

"Gee, I never thought about it like that Sandra."

"I know. I am just giving explanation to what is happening. It is my wish for people to understand and accept the experiences that are coming to them with an inquisitive mind. Not a fearful one. Oprah, Heaven is happening here on earth. We have already been told in the Bible that the souls of the past would be the first to rise. Well…."

"Well, this is it. It's kind of spooky Sandra."

"I know. It wigs me out too when it happens. But now I just get more excited and inquisitive about who is paying me a visit and what are they here to tell me?"

You could have heard a pin drop. Instead all that you could hear was the sound of the wind blowing in the trees. Oprah finally had the courage to speak.

"So, this is now the beginning of Heaven on Earth?"

"Right."

"God calling us Home is God placing Himself inside of us all."

"Yes."

"O.K." she said as she placed her hands on the chair and raised herself up onto her feet. I think that it's time I visited the little girl's room once more and have a mini break. I got up out of my chair as well and quickly added, "Sounds like a plan."

Chapter Nine

Within a few minutes we were back in our chairs and we quickly resumed our conversation. I could tell that Oprah had time to reflect on our conversation by the nature of her next question.

"Sandra, in your book you spoke of clearing out your past?"

"Yes."

"That in order to accomplish this, you went for therapy?"

"Right. I did indeed."

"How did that unfold Sandra?"

Oprah was now leaning forward in her chair and not waiting for an answer, fired another question at me.

"And why did you need to go for therapy? Was there something bothering you? How long were you in therapy?"

Taken back with her direct nature, and number of questions, I took in a breath and answered slowly as to soften the pace.

"One question at a time Oprah! Calm down girlfriend, we have got all day here!"

I moved around in my chair getting comfortable for what was to be another recounting of an amazing story.

"Yes, there was. Around 1989 I was going through a pretty rough time and I was in emotional pain. I had decided that I needed help to deal with my sadness. So, I decided to see a therapist. You know what I discovered Oprah?"

“What?”

“That healthy people seek help when they do not have all the answers. People who do not seek answers or solutions for their problems, stay stuck in their stuff. It is actually a healthier mind that realizes one has limitations and that we are not meant to go it alone.”

“In truth Sandra” Oprah said solemnly, “People usually make fun of someone else’s pain because they are either jealous or in pain themselves. It takes great courage to look deep into your own soul.”

“So many people are afraid of what they may find lurking beneath the blanket of the past.”

“You’re talking about abuse.” It was a statement and not a question.

“Yes. That is what most people are afraid that they might find. Not on a conscious level mind you. But under the surface. It is perhaps one of our greatest fears. That and not being worthy enough to be called Home to God.”

Then I looked up at her, smiled and added.

“And you my dear. I seem to recall you mentioning a time or two about the challenges you faced in your past.”

Oprah sighed and nodded her head.

“It’s not a memory I choose to think about in my present anymore.”

“Amen. Oprah. Amen.” Was she shutting the door on that subject? I wondered. So I decided to take it slow. I looked around and as a new thought entered my mind, I disclosed it to her.

"A deeper truth that lies beneath the discovery of abuse, is it is actually God calling you to know Him. For I have discovered Oprah, that the more I came to know myself, the more I came to know God. The two are so closely intertwined with one another."

"You mean the discovering of your past abuse is actually a call by God to come to know Him?"

"Yes. Know Thyself And You Shall Know God." It's an impossible journey without Him." I paused for effect... then continued...

"When a person hits a really tough patch in their lives, and this doesn't just apply to the discovery of past abuse, but any rough patch. It could be a death or an accident. Then look to this event as an opportunity to reach out to God. It is His way of calling you to come and find Him."

"So, it's actually is a GOOD thing when we experience pain or suffering."

"Crazy as it sounds. It is a signal to you that God is at your door!"

"Yes. Like an invitation to a party that you would really like to get out of!"

This time I butted in with, "Only you know you gotta go!" We both laughed at this and then Oprah said, "Ahhh what a little humor can do to lighten the conversation."

"It sounds mixed up when you hear it, but in truth, it does make a lot of sense."

"God is telling you 'I am here for you!' So, call out to Him. Simply ask." And here I raised my hands up into the air and yelled out loud.

"Hey God. What's happening? Send me some help with this!"

Oprah, taking this to be a fun exercise immediately mimicked me and also shouted out, "Same as her!" We had a mutual smile exchange and I then said, "Only, there is something that YOU must also do Oprah."

"And what may I ask is that?"

"Love yourself enough to believe that you are so loved by Him, He would never forsake you. Oprah, God never refuses one of His own. Just believe, inside of your core that once you ask Him for help, He WILL be there."

"So trying to resolve an issue no matter how big or how small simply ask Him for help because the truth is we are not meant to do this alone" Oprah quickly added.

"It's one of the key insights. So, I will reiterate it again. We are not meant to walk the road to recovery alone. Once you begin to reach out for help, you will most certainly be led. That is God's promise to us all. Hold Him to it!"

"Exactly, Oprah!" We paused and smiled at each other. Oprah then continued to recap, "So, you went to a therapist for help in order to heal from your sadness?"

"Yes, and to release past held emotions."

"You're talking about your own abuse now, are you not Sandra?"

"Yes. I am."

"How long did this take you? To clear out your closet, so to speak?"

"Years. I started in and around 1988. However, once you start down that yellow brick road that leads you to your healing, you begin to realize after a while, that this journey isn't going to end. It is the journey that is the rest of your life."

"I second that Sandra. You know when I was beginning my healing journey, I wanted the hard stuff to be over as soon as possible."

"Such as..." I inquired. "Well, the anger and pain part. You can't go around it, over it, or under it. The only way is through it."

"Then you can get on with the rest of your life. You know Sandra, it's funny how you discover that it isn't about the rushing through things to get to the finish line. Somewhere along the road, it occurs to you that this is your life and part of your time spent here is meant to be invested in discovering yourself. All of yourself."

"The good... the bad..." And we both said at the same time, "And the ugly". And we began to laugh.

I was the first to speak then. "Releasing the past Oprah, makes room in you for the future. Staying stuck in past pain or harboring resentment. That is some nasty stuff."

"I hear you girlfriend" Oprah echoed.

"Hey Oprah, you just called me girlfriend. You know, I was really waiting for you to speak those words to me."

"You were???"

"Yeah. I am not sure just as yet, who it is that I was to you in a past life."

"Or lives??????"

I smiled at that and then echoed, “Or past liiiiivvvvveeessss.” Then I continued, “But I feel so close to you. As if we were close girlfriends or sisters. Or something!”

There was a pause as I waited for spirit to offer up the knowing of it to us. After a moment I uttered a “Uhmmmph. I guess the answer to that will come when we are meant to know it!”

Oprah acknowledged this with a head nod. I went on to say, “Healing from past hurts is never an easy road to take. Not all of us will experience this in the exact same way. However, my path took me away from my first family for about twenty years.”

“That must have hurt you deeply.” Oprah sympathized.

“Yes. For two reasons. One, I couldn’t figure out why not one of my family members was sympathetic to my cause. Like why didn’t one of them believe me? Secondly, I was so alone on this journey. Having to walk away from the life I knew to forge a new one.” I just breathed out with a heavy sigh.

“I bet you missed them on holidays and family get-togethers.”

“Of course I did. However, working it out would have meant recanting what I remembered living through. It was more important for me to stand my ground and defend what my inner child had revealed to me to be true, than it was for me to stay in a situation that was still abusive.”

“I think anytime that you are not taken seriously, overlooked or objectified then it’s abusive.”

“It discounts you.”

“Like a five and dime store. I am sure that took incredible courage and strength for you to stand alone, Sandra."

I smiled back at her and said, "I am sure that there was meaning behind it, otherwise, things would not have happened the way that they did. It took years of work. I attended many workshops and seminars. Heck I went through about four therapists in order to finally release the anger and get down to the hurt and the sadness that I had been holding onto."

"Oh I know that anger! I know that anger, sugar! I had lots of it!"

I was shaking my head up and down affirming her confession.

"Oprah, I used to have this punching bag down in my basement and I would put an imaginary picture, or sometimes even an actual picture of the person who had abused me on it. Then, I would just beat the snot out of the bag, hitting it with anything from a plastic bat or hockey stick to my bare hands. Heavy rap music works best. (cause my anger surfaces real fast when I listen to that stuff) and I would yell and scream and use every angry swear word in the world and just get out my rage."

"What about your kids and your husband? Didn't they hear you?"
"Well, I had the music blaring but I tried my best to do this when I was alone in the house."

Oprah's eyes were wide open and she was listening intently to me. She then confessed, "I used to take a pillow and lock myself in my bedroom and just cry and wail!"

"Yeah? Good girl. Did that work well for you?"

"I also journal a lot and I wrote angry letters to my abusers and then never mailed them."

"Yeah, all those things really help when you're trying to get it all out of you. It took me about two years to get through the anger part."

“Just two?”

I looked at her and then took in a deep breath as I gave that some thought.

“Yeah, You’re right. Now that I think of it, I was angry for a long time. A very long time.”

Oprah raised her eyebrows looking at me with that “Who do you think you’re kidding here?” look. “O.K. O.K, Twenty years angry” I confessed.

Oprah was shaking her head up and down in affirmation.

Here I looked away from Oprah. And I paused as I collected myself, remembering. I spoke then.

“I think I held onto my anger for so long Oprah because it’s all I knew to do. It was a part of me and it allowed me to stay stuck in the “poor me” mindset.

“What do you mean Sandra?”

“Well, you know, poor me, feel sorry for me I was abused as a child and this is my story.”

“Sandra, you sound as if you are mocking the process of recovery?”

“I am not mocking the process Oprah. On the contrary, I am being honest about how devastating and encompassing this process really is. Oprah, it was not enough that I had to release my anger through all those therapeutic methods, I had to come to a realization that I was holding onto it like a prize.”

“Like a prize? What do you mean by that Sandra?”

"Oprah, I felt entitled to be angry, after all." And here I stood up on my feet and with my arms, gestured broadly. "This person did this to me and this person did this to me. And my family abandoned me and on and on." And after all that, I am left standing, holding onto my anger. I won and I am right. I have a right to be angry!"

"Well you do have a right to be angry. You should be angry at what happened to you. I know I am."

"That is exactly what I am trying to tell you. I was still hurting myself with my anger because I felt justified in having it."

"I don't follow."

"You see Oprah, for a long time, I was more interested in who was to blame for my suffering and didn't think to understand, that I WAS still suffering. My abuse as a child was over, but I was still suffering."

"Oh, I get you. You're telling me that you were still hurting from being angry, even though the actual physical abuse had ended?"

"Yes! Yes! You're getting it. I clapped my hands together in recognition of this and continued, "I would have done something to stop my suffering sooner, only it was kept from my sight."

"Why?"

"Because I was getting something out of it. I got to hold onto my story about being abused. I got to play the 'poor me'. The victim. I was an unwilling victim to adults as a child so, I cast myself the 'poor me' role for the rest of my life."

"But why would you do that to yourself, Sandra?"

"Cause it was all I knew. It was my pattern laid out for me at the on-set of my life. Oprah - that too is the tragedy of abuse. It casts you throughout your life to play a victim."

We both let this truth simmer in a little before I added, "Now Oprah, I was not conscious at the time I was doing this. It was learned behavior."

"Yes."

"I also hear you tell me that you were stuck playing the victim because it is the only way you knew how to act."

"You heard right. The wildest thing though Oprah, I didn't SEE THIS about myself. I had to learn it."

"If you are too busy pointing the blame out there" and here Oprah raised her arm and pointed as she continued to explain to me. "then, you can't look for the answers" And here Oprah pointed her right index finger inwards towards her heart chakra, "In here."

"Well said, my friend. Well said. You are right on the money. And you know what Oprah? I finally realized that I too was responsible for causing pain to others. While I was busy playing the victim role with a fistful of entitled anger, I could not see how my actions were also hurting others."

"How so?"

"O.K., I hurt my family because they could not see my reality. Cause they saw things differently because they had a different view of reality."

"Yes. They could not see my plight because they were not meant to. They only saw a family member who was making outlandish accusations against parents, friends and family. They honestly thought I was a liar."

"Or crazy."

"Yeah, that too. But actually, they could only perceive me as such. I wasted a lot of time and energy getting angry over that which simply was."

"Alright, explain that one."

"If it was their reality not to see, I could not make them."

"O.K. then Sandra, even if they couldn't see you or sympathize with you" I cut her off mid-sentence.

"It was up to me to do this work for me. It had nothing to do with them. It is about my spirit. If I wish to love and honor me, then I am to look after me and my journey. True awareness comes to you Oprah when you take responsibility for your own healing journey and not try to make it anyone else's. Oprah, once I could see more than them, I had to honor them and let go of all the pain and hurt that we have caused one another through ignorance."

"Ignorance?"

"They were unaware of my pain. But it even goes deeper Oprah. If they did not participate in my play and act exactly as they did to me, my abusers included, then I could not have made the journey towards my soul's healing."

"O.K. Sandra, now I just hear you excusing everyone who has treated you badly."

"Not excusing them. But not judging them either. Everyone is exactly who it is that they need to be in order to make the journey they need to take. I could not be where I am on my journey if I had not created or drawn to me the people in my life in order to make it all happen."

“That is some heavy stuff there Sandra.”

“Yeah, and it even gets better. Now that I finally got it that me being mad or angry at anyone who is being just the way they are supposed to be, it is actually showing me my inability to accept what is. The more I let go of trying to change or fix another, the more I can be free of them.”

“I am going to have to let this sink in a bit more. Honestly Sandra, do you have any liquor? Because right about now I could use a stiff drink!

With that I got up and I said to Oprah, “You know what girlfriend? I have a pitcher of your favorite cranberry martini’s cooling in the refrigerator right now!”

Needless to say, Oprah’s eyes lit up right away and she responded with enthusiasm, “I am two steps behind you Sandra!”

We both jumped up out of our chairs and made our way into the cottage where I had the martini glasses laid out on a tray. Oprah visited the ladies room and I carried the tray outside where I began to poor us a cool long one. She appeared shortly and after I handed her a glass, she took a sip and exclaimed.

“Ahhhhhhh! Heaven at last. I don’t know if you’re gonna stop talking long enough Sandra so I can actually enter into Heaven today, but this, is an awfully good start!

Chapter Ten

Oprah and I just took some time to just be. We sat and drank and listened contently to the breeze blowing the leaves of the very mature trees that surrounded the patio. And once again, we engaged in conversation.

"Oprah, in The Bible we hear of Jesus helping the blind men to see. I mean there may have been cases of Christ actually physically healing people, but…"

"But what Sandra?"

"But I think there was more to it. I think that what The Bible is really saying is that Christ helped men actually "SEE THEMSELVES".

Oprah's eyes lit right up! Like she was receiving an insight of the greatest magnitude.

"Sandra, you're telling me that in The Bible when it speaks of Jesus healing the blind, that he was actually restoring their inward sight?"

"Yes, yes Oprah. That is exactly it. Christ was removing the blinders we put upon ourselves unknowingly, that caused us not to see OURSELVES!"

"Gosh. Now that I am thinking of this, I see the wisdom in what you are saying to me."

"There's more. If we are blind to ourselves, we are also blind to others."

"O.K." Oprah spoke slowly.

"Oprah, how can I expect to see others as they truly are, if I cannot see myself?"

"You can't."

"No. You cannot. Not until you can see yourself. That whole analogy in The Bible about before you reach out and remove that stick out of my eye, remove first the log in yours?"

"Yeah, I know the one you mean."

"Well, same thing. Again it is Christ telling us that we must first see ourselves as we truly are. Have compassion for ourselves."

Then Oprah immediately added, "Before you can begin to have compassion for others."

Just as quickly, I asked her, "Because why Oprah? Because why?"

"Because, if I can have enough compassion towards me for being blind to my true self, then I can have compassion towards another when I recognize that they are still stuck, still being blind."

"I know I always thought that. That it was referring to an actual physical blindness. So, Sandra, why did God make us all so blind?"

"Such a great question Oprah. Because it is in the coming of the knowing of God into your life that allows you to SEE!!! Get it Oprah? You can only see yourself and remove your own blindness if you first seek out Christ and God. For it is only through Christ that you will receive that inward sight!"

"And if you do not?"

"Well, then. I guess you'll have trouble seeing the wisdom that we have just spoke of."

"Sandra, Sandra, Sandra." Oprah spoke these words in a big breath in.

"I just am blown away with this conversation we are having. I have to really think about what we were just discussing."

"Oprah, do not think for one moment I am making light of abuse. Nor am I removing a person's right to be angry with an abuser. I am also not condoning abuse of any kind. My message is for those who are seeking a way out of the blame game. People who are blaming their life circumstances on others. Refusing to seek out help for themselves because it's easier to stay stuck in anger and resentment."

"And entitlement."

"Especially entitlement."

"O.K. Oprah paused and slowly said, "I Gotcha."

"Oprah, it is so amazing to me that in our times, we have so discounted God and His power. It's like, who wouldn't want to tap into this? It is such a cool road to walk down and once you have, He places into you such a desire to tell others."

"Only how come so many people can't hear this? Or laugh at it or mock it?" I butted in with, "Or just plain dismiss it. They dismiss it! And that's what really gets me Oprah is they dismiss something that is the foundation of our existence here. Our purpose for living. Our soul's main reason to reincarnate into the physical realm. It is to make this journey."

"So how come so many people miss it?"

"I only have one answer for you, Oprah. It is because they were not meant to see the path. It is hidden from their view."

"Because God made them blind?"

"No. Because God gave us a choice to stay blind or have sight."

"Well, how can you receive sight?"

"First, you must seek God out and He will reward you with it. Cause really Oprah, that is one of the gifts Christ gave to us. He makes Blind Men and Women see. End of story."

"I am hearing you speak of this today Sandra as if it were the first time I was hearing it."

"Really Oprah? Explain to me how you are feeling?"

"Well. It's as if I really get it. I mean, I actually do get this. I first have to seek out Christ and ask Him to help me see myself."

"Yes, that is correct." Oprah continued slowly as if we were extracting teeth.

"Then, once I ask for Him to help me see myself, He will bring things, events, and awareness to me so that I can see parts of myself that have remained hidden from me."

"Yes!"

"But Sandra, isn't it so strange because after being with me" Oprah pointed to her chest, "For the fifty-some odd years I have been with me" And here she looked over at me and smiled that "I won't tell my age and I won't ask yours" thing women have with one another the older they get. I smiled back at her and she continued, "I find it hard to imagine that there are things about myself that I still don't know. You would think after all this time spent with me, I would know me."

"Yeah. I know, it's wild isn't it? Like, I couldn't see how entitled I was to my anger until I was actually shaking my fist at some poor woman in a self-help class."

"Which class was that Sandra?"

"A class on Archetypes, by Caroline Myss."

"Oh yeah?"

"Yeah, it was in that class that Jesus helped me to see a part of myself that had remained hidden from me for twenty, no wait. All of my life."

"You're talking about the anger aren't you? That is when you discovered you still had it and that you were still causing yourself and others pain over it?"

"Yup. A lady was there in my class who was having the same problem as me only in reverse."

"I don't follow what you mean by that Sandra."

"I was angry at my mother because of the abuse in our family and I was blaming her for it."

"Where was your father?"

"Oh, he had passed on at the age of fifty."

"Fifty! That is really young."

"Yeah, I know. When I was in my teens, I thought fifty was pretty old. Now that I am in my fifties, I realize just how young my father really was when he died."

I smiled with my lips pressed together and then added,

"Anyways, at the time I directed anger at my mother." I paused and added quickly, "And Oprah, my anger was justified."

Oprah listened to me intently. "Go on" she said.

"I removed myself from her and my family environment and then surrounded myself with as many loving and supportive people that I could. In that safe environment I was able to love and nurture myself back to where I was beginning to be me again."

"And not the victim."

"Right. And not the victim. So, anyway, in this class, I was sitting across from a mother whose daughter had removed herself and her children from her life because of the abuse that existed in THEIR family. This mother was saddened. She was crying about how truly hurt and torn apart she was by this rejection from one of her daughters. The removal of her grandchildren from her own life was more than she could bear. Oprah, instead of feeling compassion for her, I sat forward and told her angry faced with hands clenched into a fist."

I took a moment to demonstrate this and then continued on with my story.

"That SHE was the adult, SHE was the one who should go after her little girl and tell her how sorry that SHE was for not protecting her child. That is was her job to keep her little girl safe and she had failed at it."

Oprah just looked at me. I was lost in the intensity of the moment as I was allowing all my true feelings to surface.

"So, what happened then?"

"So that was the moment when it hit me that I had considered myself blameless for causing another person/persons pain. I kept thinking that everyone saw the situation the same way as I did. That my way of seeing the past was the right way.”

“Well, it was the truth for you was it not, Sandra?”

“Oh yes. Definitely it was the truth in my world Oprah.”

“But not in others?”
“
No. We all have different truths Oprah for we all are in our own worlds. We perceive the world through a screen that is filtered with our memories and our learning. No two people see the world the same way.”

“That is never the case.”

“You are right Oprah!” and I paused again.

“It was a blessing in disguise for me to receive that insight into MYSELF. I was able to truly see that I was also responsible.”

“You were responsible? Am I hearing you correctly Sandra?”

“I am responsible in that we create our own world for the lessons we are here to learn. The blessing came when I realized that perhaps I now had the power to make a change. If I put aside who was right or wrong. If I let go of my justified anger. What did I have left?”

“A new story. A blank page on which to write an entirely different future for yourself and your family”

“Exactly.”

“So, what did you do?”

“I went to all of my family members and confessed my part in the problem."

"And..." Oprah lead me onto finish.

"And I was able to open a door that had long been closed off."

"So you're seeing you family again after twenty years?"

"Yup. And I have come to conclude that it was not my families' journey to clear out their karma from all the past lives of abuse in this lifetime. It was mine."

"What are you saying, Sandra?"

"I am saying to you that once the wisdom came to me that even though I was living in a family, where you would think that what was happening to one of the family members, would happen to them all."

"Not true."

"No. Not true. Even if it was, they remained blind to my plight because it was not part of their lesson to learn this lifetime!"

"Pardon me?" Oprah looked at me through squinting eyes.

"My greatest release of this entire issue came about six months ago when I discovered that the reason I was so alone on my path to recovery and why it was that I received no support from those closest to me while I was going through all of my recovery process was because it was not part of THEIR journey."

"So you're saying that they were oblivious to your pain and suffering because they were not meant to travel along the same road as you were to travel this lifetime?"

"Yes! Oprah. You got it! There was not a family member who

was sympathetic to my cause simply because they were not meant to be." I paused and looked at Oprah to see if she was registering with me by her facial expressions.

She was nodding but saying nothing, so I concluded with, "Oprah, do you realize if they had crossed that line. If but one of my sisters, my brother or my mother had reacted any differently to the disclosure I had made with regards to the path my soul was taking this lifetime. I would not have found my own strength to deal with what my soul was here to learn. Oprah, how much pain and suffering could be eliminated? How much of our energy could we conserve and protect if we just came to the realization that we need not look to others to validate our path?"

I got up from my chair now and was waving my arms and looking directly at Oprah.

"We suffer alone because we yearn for others to "GET US" – to understand what we are going through, whatever the situation. But Oprah, how can they understand us or sympathize with us or even acknowledge our pain when they are NOT MEANT TO?"

"Others can't." Oprah conceded.

I marched on. "They are BLINDED to us!"

"Those who have walked a similar path as you, would however, be able to give you that understanding." I was nodding along with her as she concluded with.

"And to offer you support."

"Exactly. But Oprah, we are all in different realities! Everyone's minds think differently! Everyone here is on a separate mission for their soul's enlightenment. If my soul's mission this time around is to recover from all my lifetimes of abuse and yours isn't, then guess what Oprah? You and I are not gonna click. We have different jobs to do for our soul's completion. If you can keep this in the forefront of your mind, you will waste less of your time on trying to 'get along' with others who are not where you are at."

"True, Sandra. But what about families? If I understand what you are telling me, then how many of us who are in families, are ever on the same path together?"

"Good question Oprah! In fact, great question Oprah!"

"And the answer is very few. I believe, most family problems stem from the TOXIC belief that we all have to Be the same. Think the same. Act the same. Believe the same things as we were told by our parents."

"And their parents before them."

"Exactly Oprah! We need to respect each other's differences. In fact, celebrate them. Oprah, what if we all respected one another's right to be on a different path? If we accepted that everyone is exactly where they need to be" And I raised my voice for emphasis "Right now! That you were not being disrespectful or disruptive just because you approached your life's journey from a different place?" I paused here and let that one hang.

Oprah then spoke.

"So if your brother chooses to live his life as a smoker, you should let him?" I laughed out loud at that.

"Should you LET him?"

Just listen to yourself Oprah. Listen to the language you are using! "It's not about letting him, it's about respecting him. Maybe, he is on the right path to where ever he needs to be."

"Maybe he is here to experience death through lung cancer" Oprah fired back.

"Could be, or maybe at age thirty-five he decides to quit and at those quiet smoking meetings he meets up with another person who ends up befriending him and happens to like his marketing ideas, offers him a job and the next thing you know it," Oprah butted in with, "He's off on a new career and ends up going to England and meets the girl of his dreams!"

"Now you've got it Oprah, or ends up meeting the girl of his dreams. My point is, how can you know what you have got planned out for someone else's life, is the right thing for them?"

"You can't."

"No, you can't. Oprah." I paused. With a heavy sigh, I told her, "I cannot even begin to tell you the time and the energy I have wasted. Wasted. Exasperated myself on trying to change others to suit me. Trying to help others or fix them so that I could be happier."

"Hummph! It sounds so silly now. Doesn't it Sandra?"

"Silly, huh! The audacity! The arrogance! The stupidity. Why on earth did I ever think it was my right to tell another single human being how to be?"

I don't know if Oprah felt sorry for me as I was certainly feeling what I was confessing to her at this moment. She did her best to alleviate my distress.

"Maybe you were blind to it?" Oprah stated flatly. She looked at me, pressed her lips together and became quiet. The humor simply hung in the air until I eventually got it. I looked over to her nodding my head and said in an equally funny tone, "Funny lady!" I shook my head and had to laugh.

"Good one queen of day time television. Very good!"

"I thought so." She answered smugly.

"I suppose you're all high and mighty seeing that you get to lead people into a new earth this life time?"

"As opposed to a desert?"

"As opposed to a desert."

"Yeah, yeah I am."

"Being Moses certainly has its perks now doesn't it?"

"Not bad…not bad." Our little back and forth banter came to an end as Oprah quieted and then spoke.

"Sandra, you know, I am really thinking about what you have just shared with me and it is starting to make sense to me. What if over all my lifetimes my soul has experienced abuse from both sides?"

"Both sides, Oprah?"

"What if I have been an offender as well as a victim? What if during this lifetime, I too was to journey to that place where I had to heal from abuse? Which I believe I have."

"Oprah, does one ever really heal from abuse? I think it is an on-going journey. Just when you have healed one aspect of your life or your personality, Oops! Along comes another thing. I'll give you an example. You did a television show in February of this year where you had on those four guys who were convicted child molesters." Oprah let out a sigh and said.

"Yes, I remember."

"That took guts. That took so much courage for you to face those men and to remain so calm and collected."

"Thanks."

"No. Oprah. Not just thanks, WOW! I know what buttons were being pushed inside of you that you could not react to. You had to remain in the journalists chair when in truth, you were symbolically facing your perpetrators." It grew silent. I continued, "You know. I didn't even want to watch your show that day. I can remember. I was afraid. I was sickened by the thought of it. I really had to struggle to turn it on. I was offering apologies to my twenty-one year old son who was in the next room with his friend playing FIFA soccer on the Play Station. 'Oprah doesn't have a really nice show on today, but I am going to try and watch it and I may just turn it off' I told them." I let out a sigh and considered telling her what really happened for me as I viewed that broadcast. I decided to let her know how it truly did affect me. She was listening intently.

"Oprah, do you know how I felt as soon as I turned it on and saw those men, knowing who they were?"

"No."

"I am so ashamed to tell you this because I reacted to it and had no control over how I was gonna feel."

"How did you feel then Sandra?" Oprah asked, her concern overriding my embarrassment.

"My body released the energy as it does when I am sexually aroused and I wanted to run into my bedroom and masturbate."

I think I stunned her into silence with that statement and she replied, "Sandra, DO NOT FEEL ASHAMED OF HOW YOUR BODY REACTED. You were a child and your body remembered, not you."

"Thanks Oprah. I really wasn't going to tell you that, however, it was the truth. I think that my body had a trigger knowing that there were men on your show who would molest children and as a child I too, did not just have one abuser, but many."

"So seeing those men caused your body to have a flash-back." That's a statement - not a question.

"Yes. And I would go into the act. The pattern as I did when I was a little girl. What is most upsetting is that I couldn't understand where this feeling was coming from. Oprah. My grown-up mind was mortified that my body was responding, independent of me and I felt once again as if I had no control over my body."

"Just as you did when you were being molested."

"Yes. Just as I did way back then. How can it still be with me after all the therapy and all the healing work I have done?"

"Sandra, what you are telling me is that by watching my show, you became re-victimized."

"Yes, Oprah. And I think that is why I was so afraid to watch it. Perhaps on some level, I was trying to protect my inner child from becoming re-victimized by watching that show." I then looked at Oprah and seeing the look on her face I quickly added, "Oh! But that isn't your fault Oprah. I mean your intention to run that show was to help and not to harm."

"Yes" She answered.

"No, I got that. I was just so shocked that still after all that time, my body remembered how to be around abusers. It's as if it were engrained into my DNA or something."

“Interesting” Oprah pondered.

“How so?” I asked her.

“Well Sandra, you have got me thinking. If you had a reaction such as that, perhaps other woman who also watched it had similar responses.”

“None that I read on your site after the show.”

“No.”

“Lots of confessions. I didn’t read anyone’s comments that matched up with mine.”

“Why didn’t you e-mail your thoughts in?”

“I tried to only I was having trouble signing in and my password didn’t work, so, I thought if I ever got to meet you, I would tell you then.”

“Or put it in your book?”

“Yeah, that too! No. I just wanted to tell you that what that long haired man said, well, it riveted me to my chair.”

“What was that?”

“The part when you asked him if he understood what he had done and he answered that he couldn’t possibly know.”

“Which was exactly right.”

“Oh, so exactly the right answer! He could never know.”

“But the other answer that he had.”

"That he had murdered her?"

"Yeah. That was the focal point of your entire show. That was the statement right there. That was worth going through all those feelings again. Just to hear truth spoken."

"Yes. I agree with you. That is what it truly boils down to. He murdered that child. Murdered who she could have been had she not been made a victim of childhood sexual abuse."

"So sad, Sandra."

"So, so sad Oprah. So, so, very, very sad. But it was the truth. I have had to fight back my entire life the damage that was done."

"Myself as well."

"So, you and I both know that it is murder."

"That is why I wanted to do the show."

"Oprah, I truly believe that you facing those four men, as a former victim of childhood sexual abuse, well you became a channel for us all. Symbolically Oprah, you were actually facing your own abusers."

Oprah clasped her fingers together and fixed her gaze into her lap. I could tell that she was feeling what I had just told her. Silence.

Mixed emotions hung in the air. Finally she said, "Thank-you Sandra for that. Yeah, I guess you're right."

Tears were in her eyes as in mine. We both looked at one another and in an instant we were both on our feet and locked in an embrace of mutual support for one another's journey through the hell that is abuse recovery. Having both walked down that path, gave us a bond that can only be understood by another traveler. We held onto each other for comfort and for acknowledgment of the courage that it took to face our darkest demons and emerge, victorious.

Chapter Eleven

Our afternoon was moving along nicely. As women often do, one subject turns into another and pretty soon, there are three or four subjects on the go!

As Oprah and I sat out over-looking our beautiful scenery, I remembered to pick up on a subject that I began to tell her about previously.

"Now Oprah, as strange as this is, I seem to get most of my noteworthy visitations from angels and spirit around Easter." And here I paused and pressed my lips together and took in a deep breath as I geared myself up for my next story.

"Well why do you think that is Sandra?"

"I'm not sure, Oprah. But over the years I have come to think that there must be some logical explanation for it cause so much happens to me around Easter. Like, I have this crazy idea that there must be some kind of" and here I raised my hands and opened them towards the sky as I continued on, "of cosmic, terrestrial, interplanetary energies being produced during Easter that seem to lift up my energy and in turn this opens me up to receive spiritual messages more intensely and more frequently than other times of the year."

"Really? Go on." Oprah enticed me further to explain my true thinking.

"And then at other times, I think it is because at Easter time, most of us here on the earth, are all focusing our energy and our intentions upon Christ and this raises up the world's vibration and I pick up on it."

"Sandra, that is really cool." Oprah seemed fascinated at my attempts to explain my heightened spiritual awareness during Easter time.

“Yeah. It is really cool. Anyways, I can remember praying one afternoon on Good Friday in 1988 and asking God to take away the pain I was feeling during my recovery process and replace it with the peace that Christ felt on the cross. The peace that comes when we release our will, and ask that God's will be done instead. It's a surrendering to the will of God.”

I then looked right in Oprah's eyes and said, “Oprah, it was amazing because no sooner had I asked for that peace, when it came upon me and all of a sudden I became so calm. So calm and so full of peace that if they could have bottled it and sold it, millions would be made!”

"Really?”

“Truly Oprah, it was on that day that I felt Christ’s spirit for the first time in me. It was as if He was paying me a visit and the gift that He brought me was the feelings that He himself had felt on the cross. It was truly amazing because this holiness, this familiarity enveloped me and I knew exactly how He had felt.”

“So, you are telling me Sandra that when Jesus was on the cross He did not feel frightened or sad?”

“I am telling you Oprah that Christ felt nothing but a peaceful calm and acceptance of what was. He was not arguing or cursing or lamenting. None of that. Oprah, it was God who gave Him that peace. It was God who placed it in me so that I could know it.”

“That is pretty cool Sandra.”

“Yeah, I know. It was so cool when it happened, I will never forget it.”

"Yeah, and it is also cool that you asked God for it and you got it right away!"

"Yeah, I know that part was also great! Oprah, it's like that for me almost every Easter. Something, Godly or spiritual is usually taking place for me. I LOVE it!" Oprah and I sat and laughed.

"So, go on Sandra!"

"O.K. so, then after that presence came into me, I could talk with God. (It was not the same intensity as in 1994), however, I began to hear this voice inside my head and this voice would tell me to write things down."

Oprah immediately sat up a little straighter and said, "Oh. What were you directed to write Sandra?"

"Well stuff about Christ and being the Light, and all sorts of stuff. It was as if I was just taking dictation from the voice. I was being commanded to write it down."

"And did you?"

"Well, I really had no choice you see because it was such a strong, overpowering feeling of urgency that, yes, when I heard it, I obeyed. Where ever I was when I heard the voice command me, I got up and I wrote down what it told me. Now Oprah, this started to happen to me at night time and then pretty soon, it started in the day time as well!"

Oprah just kept nodding at me to go on.

"In fact, I kept an ongoing dairy and in it were these channeling's I call them, interspersed with my own personal feelings regarding this entire situation I had found myself in. Now, Oprah, get this…" I leaned over the table between us and looked right at her, "You see, after this voice was in me, a lot of cool stuff began to happen. I found out that I also had developed the ability to Heal."

"Do you mean hands on healing?" She led me on.

"Yes. Healing arts such as Polarity. Reiki. Both involving energy which is emitted out from the palms of your hands." And here I held out my hands and showed her with my right hand drawing a circle on the center of my left palm.

"Here, is the strongest point on both your hands." I had Oprah hold out her hands as well and I drew a circle on her palms and continued to explain further.

"Now Oprah, this is where the energy comes out of and to really feel this, take your two hands and rub them together really fast so that you can begin to feel a friction between them."

Both of us did this together. When I felt that she was getting it, I directed her to stop and then to close her eyes and place both palms facing one another in front of her. Oprah complied with this and I then said, "Good. Now see if you can begin to feel the warmth between your palms."

"Oh I can! I can!" she seemed very pleased with this.

"O.K. now imagine that there is this giant cotton ball between your hands." I gave her time to feel it and before you knew it her hands began to move apart.

"My hands feel like they are floating Sandra."

I was delighted to see how well this was working.

"Oprah, open your eyes and look at where your hands are now!"

Oprah opened her eyes only to see that her hands had moved about a foot apart from one another. I could tell by her expression that she was marveling at this tiny miracle.

"Sandra, why is this happening?"

"You are emitting a powerful energy Oprah out of the palms of your hands. We all have it."

"We all have this?"

"Yeah. And when you take your hands and place them…" I paused and reached over and placed her hands on the opposite side of her left leg. Now close your eyes again and see if you can visualize the energy moving from one hand through your leg and into the other hand."

I waited as she concentrated on the task at hand. Pretty soon, this big wide white smile appeared on her face as she exclaimed to me.

"Oh my heavens Sandra, now my leg is warm as well!"

"That's because the healing energy from your hands is now moving through your leg.

"And everyone can do this?"

"Everyone can do this."

"So what is this good for?"

"Well this is called Reiki and it is a powerful healing tool that can work miracles. Your see if moves energy in the body. Sometimes if we have an injury, the energy remains fixed, or stuck in that area. This Reiki allows for the blockages to be removed and begins again the natural flow of energy in the body."

"So now I can do Reiki!"

"Now you can do Reiki. Only, there are courses to take and attunements to the Reiki Masters to be made."

"Attunements?"

"It simply means that you align yourself, or become a willing channel for this healing energy to work through you. If you are interested in learning more about it, let me know and I can set you up with a Reiki Master Healer who teaches this and can show you more."

"Neat. Sandra, thanks for showing me this. So, do you do anything more?"

"Well, yes, I am a licensed Yoga Instructor."

"So do you teach yoga?"

"Yes, I have taught yoga for the past fourteen years. Many of my days have been spent up here practicing yoga and creating my own postures" I offered as I looked around the grounds.

"Take for example right here Oprah." I walked over to the railing.

"This railing is fantastic for stretching!"

Oprah just nodded.

"I so love to practice yoga Oprah, It is the only exercise that embodies mind, body and spirit."

"And we all know that you are all about the spirit!"

"Right you are Oprah. And I think that I recall that you are also a

Reflexologist?"

"Yes. Yes that as well."

"That's when you heal a person by rubbing their feet" Oprah offered.

I chuckled a bit at this and smiled as I answered.

"That is also correct."

"I luuuuuv to get my feet rubbed! Mmmm, Mmmm!" She immediately turned her chair and held her feet up to me. We both smiled. How could I refuse? This was Oprah in front of me! Of course I offered!

"Fine, here, give them to me." I faked a hesitant, well if you insist tone of voice.

I placed one foot on my lap and instructed her that I would do one foot at a time while I was telling her my story.

"It actually heals the body weather you believe in it or not." I stated.

"Just keep talking Sandra, because as long as you're rubbing, I'm still listening."

Chapter Twelve

Next, I wanted to share with Oprah how it was I learned about a past life of my own. I began by telling her this:

"Oprah, I first began to practice yoga at a fitness center that I had been going to for a number of years. I enjoyed it immensely because it helped me to learn how to breathe and bring calm into my centre before reacting angrily to demanding two year olds!"

We both laughed at that!

"Along the way I had become quite fond of my teacher who was very talented. She not only taught yoga, Polarity and Reflexology, but she also held meditation classes."

"I have always wanted to learn more about meditation Sandra! I know that they say it is so good for you!"

"In more ways than you can imagine Oprah. But these particular classes that my yoga teacher was holding in home were way cool. I loved them!"

"I can tell you did. What was so special about them?"

"Well, they weren't your average meditation classes."

"No, how so?"

"Well, for one thing, they were based on the teachings of Native American Indians."

Oprah's eyebrows raised and she said, "Not Indian, from India classes?"

"Far from it! Now, don't get me wrong, we still meditated by sitting in a circle and having quiet time to connect with our inner selves and all, but I really learned how it is that Native Indians connected to what they call Great Spirit."

"O.K?" Oprah looked as if she needed a bit more of an explanation. I obliged her.

"Native Indians communicated more with God or Great Spirit as they call it, by watching and interacting with the world around them. They studied the animals and nature."

"I see."

"Yeah, so these meetings were neat. We got to smudge ourselves and cleanse our auras and read Animal Cards. Fun stuff. One time we actually had real Native Indians in for a ceremony and that was really awesome Oprah!"

"I would think that it would be. I love to learn new things all the time, Sandra."

"I do too Oprah. Learning more about the way Native Indians honor Mother Earth and all that she does for us, well, it humbles you. You begin to realize just how precious all of life truly is."

I looked deep into Oprah's eyes and said.

"We are all so connected to one another. It just really opened my eyes to that fact." And I paused and took in another deep breath. I realized I had gotten of topic again and said, "Anyways, I will get into that more later on if you are interested. I am getting sidetracked from my story."

"O.K., O.K., O.K. Go on" Oprah insisted.

"One weekend, we all went up north for a Healing Retreat at her property. She owned some land up north and had built a really nice home on it. So, a bunch of us headed up there and got to participate in a “sweat lodge” ceremony on the Friday evening and got to receive healing treatments throughout the Saturday and the Sunday.”

"Sweat lodge?" Oprah questioned.

“It's a Native Indian form of detoxification and spiritual healing. It's pretty neat.”

“Humph!” was the reply. Then she asked.

“So, what do you do in a sweat lodge beside sweat” Oprah wondered.

I smiled and answered, “Pretty much that’s it. You sweat. You sweat a lot in fact because you’re in this tiny space, a tent like thing and they keep on bringing in these hot rocks. And you sing or chant these Native songs at the same time you are sweating out all your toxins and negativity.”

“It doesn’t sound like much fun to me, Sandra.”

“Well, maybe not. But it certainly makes you feel light as a feather when you’re done!” Oprah just looked at me as if to say, “Well, whatever turns you on.”

“Soooooo.” I was sounding frustrated trying to get back to the main story here! I stopped and then started.

“The following morning when we got up, there were to be treatments given to all the participants.”

“Reiki?”

“Yes as a matter of fact Oprah, It was Reiki treatments that they were offering.”

"So, I got to go first. And it was really funny because I had a strong feeling during breakfast, that I would be the first to receive that day. And you know what Oprah? I was right. We ended up picking numbers that morning to see who would in fact, be the first, second, third and so on, and I did end up picking number one!"

"So, you were right weren't you Sandra. It's funny that you knew it before it happened. So, what happened during your treatment?"

"I ended up being worked upon by two women at the same time."

"You can do that?" Oprah was quick to ask.

"Oh yeah. I have even had treatments where there have been three people treating one person at the same time. The benefit of this is that you are on the healing table for a shorter time and it can be very powerful." Oprah nodded as I continued on.

"Anyways, it was during that session, I was told in a past lifetime I was a Roman Soldier."

"They did past life readings?"

"Yes. It just happened to come up during my hands on body treatment."

"Is that a usual thing for that to happen?"

"Well, I have learned over the years that the more in touch with spirit your practitioner is, well then you never know what can happen! It also depends upon the person receiving the treatment too Oprah."

"How so?"

"If you are open to spirit's healings and messages then you may get more messages."

"And that day you got more than just a Reiki treatment?"

"Yes, I got a past life reading as well."

"And these ladies who were practicing Reiki on you also told you that in a previous life time that you were once a Roman Soldier?"

"Well, as it turns out Oprah, not just any Roman Soldier." And I paused for effect, then announced, "It turns out that I am the Roman Soldier that had pierced Christ's side on the cross!" Oprah's eyebrows went way up with that disclosure!

"Say what?" Oprah cried.

"You heard me. The Roman Soldier that in history was the one that had to spear Christ's side in order to make sure that he was dead." There was silence now, while Oprah took this in. I went on, "Yup, it was a lot for me to take in at the time as well. I mean really, Oprah, what are you supposed to do with that information?"

Oprah did not even attempt to answer the question at all. I think she needed a moment to process what she had just heard. Finally she said to me,

"I wouldn't know what to do with that information, Sandra."

"Well I didn't either Oprah. So, I decided to go for a walk. Honestly, I remember walking in the woods and feeling, well, sad and yet detached from all the emotions that such a discovery of self, would entail. I heard it, but I still was unable to integrate this newly revealed information about one of my past lives."

"I should think so! Were you ever able to get in touch with that part of your soul's journey?"

After hearing that last question, I was also somewhat amazed at Oprah. She was certainly holding her own asking such insightful and pertinent questions. I guess you don't get to her station in life by not knowing how to conduct a proper interview! I answered her question, "As a matter of fact, yes I was able to get in touch a little bit more with that past life time of mine at a later date, when I …" Oprah cut me off with another quick observation.

"Sandra, you know I can't help but be somewhat amazed that you were such a, well" Oprah was searching for the words, then her eyes lit up "Villain. One of the bad guys who helped to crucify Jesus." She paused only to continue.

"To be present, to actually be there at the time of Christ's crucifixion, and then to find out the role you played. Well, quite frankly," Then it was my turn to cut her off mid-sentence.

"Look Oprah, it wasn't that easy for me to get my head around this either. And yes, I struggled with being the bad guy. I will confess, that I saw my picture up there on The Great Villains' Throughout History Wall of Fame, right alongside Uncle Adolf."

Oprah laughed at my joke.

"But then after awhile, I began to realize that our souls have experienced all things. Being both the hero and the bad guy. And remember too Oprah, Christ's death was a necessary evil."

"How so?"

"Christ had to die Oprah, so that we all could live."

Oprah's head was shaking up and down in silent affirmation as I expanded upon my point.

"I was just following the orders given to me. And remember too, at the time, Christ was not who He is today. In many eyes, He was a radical. Chances are that in the eyes of a soldier of the state, He was just another man that had to be put to death by crucifixion."

"I suppose that you're right about that." She sat there and thought about that for a minute. Scratched her chin and then said, "I guess so."

"Not only that, but that there was meaning behind that past lifetime of mine."

"Like what?"

"Like if I hadn't had that puzzle piece given to me, then I would not have been able to understand the important role I am to play in this life time."

"Put it together for me Sandra."

"I will, but for now, I want to explain to you, how the knowledge of this past life time, being the Roman Soldier, led me into an entirely cool adventure." Oprah took a sip of her drink and then after returning her glass to the table said, "So, go on Sandra, I am listening."

Chapter Thirteen

"Being the Roman Soldier took on a greater meaning for me about six months later. Again, this story happened at Easter time."

I gave a moment for Oprah to get the meaning of this. She acknowledged the significance of this by affirming to me, "Easter time again. Got it."

I smiled and continued.

"I was working at a therapy clinic on the Lakeshore in Clarkson. There were two massage therapists, three osteopaths, a doctor of acupuncture, a shiatsu therapist, a receptionist and myself."

"And what were you doing then?"

"Teaching yoga and doing both Reiki and Reflexology." Oprah nodded in acknowledgment.

"So, on the weeks coming up to Easter that year, I can remember having an uncanny desire to be with the people that I was working with and to hold a meditation party or something on the Good Friday."

"For everyone in your office?"

"No, just some, as well as a few of my own personal friends. It was strange Oprah, but the personal friends of mine, for some reason, all ended up pulling out at the last minute. I decided to cancel the party."

"Well what was strange?"

"What was strange was that I should not have cancelled the entire get-together. Looking back upon it Oprah, I believed my personal friends cancelled because they weren't supposed to be there!"

"Oh, you mean they weren't gonna come cause they weren't supposed to?"

"Yeah, now you got it! Only at the time, I didn't clue into that. I just threw the baby out with the bath water."

"Yeah, you cancelled the entire party and what you should have done was just let it be."

"Yup. And I know this to be true because, as soon as Good Friday drew near, I had this overwhelming feeling that I had to be with my fellow workers."

"Hummmmm" Oprah said as she was intently following along.

"No, seriously, Oprah. It was so very strong, this feeling."

Oprah interrupted me, "The feeling that you had to see your fellow co-workers?"

"Right. The feeling was literally pulling me to go into the office so that I could "Be" with these people.

"So, you're saying that this pull you felt to be with your co-workers from the therapy clinic caused you to go and be with them anyways, even though you cancelled the party?"

"Yes. I remember driving down to the office and on my way, I began to feel a presence upon me. It was so, STRONG, Oprah. It was not unlike that voice, that God's voice, that I would hear and I would have to write down what it was telling me. Only this time, it was a feeling of urgency. So, it was at this time, on this day that I began to learn to speak with the voice and not just obey it."

"Because up until now you had just obeyed the voice. You did not have a conversation with it."

"Yes. I remember most of the conversation that day and it was something like, 'Why is it so important God for me to be seeing these people of all times, Easter Weekend? Does this have anything to do with me being the Roman Soldier?' and Oprah, my head began to move forward as if to acknowledge that the answer was a yes."

"Sandra, that is really cool. Go on."

"So, when the answer was No, my head would move back. So, now I had a way of speaking to this presence and I began to ask questions. Like, were the people in my office also present at the time of Christ? My head went forward. Yes. Did they know Jesus? Yes. Who were they? Then I was told that my fellow workers consisted of Simon-Peter, Christ's best friend, Mary Magdalene, Jaraius and His daughter, a prostitute, another roman soldier and a powerful figure in the Jewish community who helped to organize the death of Jesus."

"Oh my! So, now that you knew who it is that they all were in a past lifetime, were you thinking of telling them?"

"Well, let's just say that when I got there I was not exactly sure what I was to do with this information. And you know what Oprah?"

"What?"

"And this is the weird part. Amazingly, when I go there, no clients were in the office. Now Oprah, that is very unusual to have absolutely all the therapists free at one time. I took this to be a sign. So…"

"So what did you do Sandra?"

"I rounded them up and I sat them all down in the front of the office. First, I told them my story about finding out that I was the Roman Soldier and then I told them one by one, who each of them were at the time of Jesus' life."

Oprah was certainly sitting there wide eyed! I kept on talking cause I was on a roll!

"They all shook their heads in amazement as I matched each one of them up to a past life."

"Sandra, that is amazing!"

"I know. And Oprah, what was really wild is how their present life circumstances and personalities all seemed to correspond to their past life time two thousand years ago!"

"Sandra, that is amazing! How did they take this?"

"Well, Oprah, it's kind of the same way I felt when I found out that I was the Roman Soldier. You hear it and you do your best to integrate it, however, it takes time before the meaning of it sinks in."

I smiled at Oprah, "How's your foot feeling?"

"Wonderful! It's a little tender on the instep though."

"That's your adrenal area. Take in a nice deep breath and I'll just hold my finger on it for a minute. Breathe. Good. Now just try to breathe and relax while I do the rest of your foot. I continued on with the foot treatment and the subject at hand.

"So, go on with the story, Sandra" Oprah urged me.

"After I told everyone who it was that they were in a past lifetime, they seemed to accept what it was that I told them. In fact, I think that they all thought it was kind of neat."

"Well that in itself is something. I mean that the people you worked with were so open to hearing about this. No one laughed at it or thought it was unbelievable?"

"If they did, they kept it to themselves. No, Oprah, I think they all thought it was really cool!"

"What about you Sandra? How were you feeling at the time getting this information? It must have taken you by surprise that all of a sudden you would know peoples' past lives?"

"Yeah. You're right Oprah, I was just as freaked out as the rest of them when I not only received this information, but had the courage to tell them all about it!"

"Were you at all hesitant to reveal this information?"

"Yeah, for sure I was. Only, at the time, the energy in the office was so high."

"Meaning?"

"Well, it was like it was meant to be. You know Oprah when you're in the flow of spirit, one thing naturally leads to another."

"Just don't come from fear or the flow will stop."

"Right. And in this case, I decided to trust what I was doing and what spirit was guiding me to do."

"Bravo Sandra. That took guts."

"Yes it did, but afterwards, I knew I had done the right thing."

"How so?"

“Cause it felt right. Kind of like being in this energy and just following it. Like it was so meant to happen.”

“I think I get it.”

“I know you would Oprah! It is soooo great that you are open to hearing about this and learning new stuff. I look at the world of spirit as our new “Undiscovered Country”.

“It is, isn’t it, Sandra? We know so much about the world but too little about ourselves.”

“Soon to be rectified my dear!”

“Gotcha!”

“So what else I want to tell you Oprah, is this: It was not just the people in my office that I knew whose souls were in a past life”

“No?” Oprah’s eyebrows moved upwards.

“I also began to know who others were in their past lives as well.”

“Like who?”

“Like my yoga students and personal friends. It almost seemed at the time, just about everyone whom I ran into, seemed to have been alive around the time of Jesus. Coincidence? I don't think so.”

“So you’re telling me Sandra that people were coming to you from all aspects of life, who also were there when Jesus was alive? What do you think that meant?” Oprah asked.

“Oprah, to be honest, I seriously began to think that if the people who knew Jesus were making themselves known to me now, then it could mean only one thing."

We both looked at each other and I whispered, "That He would be coming back too!"

Oprah sat up a little straighter and said in a non-believing what I just heard voice you tell me voice.

"Right."

"No, Oprah, hear me out. Spirit was bringing to me all the characters in the Christ story. From His birth, His lifetime and His death. So much so, that I began to keep a chart of who was who."

"You began a chart?"

"Yup. I would list the name of the person in the present and then who it was they were two thousand years ago. Oprah, it began to get really wild! It didn't matter where I was or where I would go. If I found myself alone with someone, and a conversation about spirituality surfaced then bingo! Before you knew it, I had another name on my chart."

"Really? And people were open to hearing about this?"

"Those who were open to spirit heard me. Those not open to spirit, just were not attracted to me. Let's just say, I would not have this kind of conversation with anyone who was not of a spiritual nature."

"And why is that?"

"Honestly Oprah, it's because the conversation just wouldn't come up."

"And that is because the universe would not bring to you those who were not on a path to discover their soul's past journeys?"

"Kind of..." I hesitated and then said.

"It has more to do with, how some people are on a path and searching for themselves. Their meaning, their purpose. They open up to all kinds of possibilities. They allow themselves to be in acceptance of the unexplainable. Of the miraculous."

"And when you are able to begin to allow those thoughts into your mind... you begin to create more unexplainable miracles in your life."

"Well I am fascinated! I can't get over how you seem to get the information on who is who. And documenting it on a chart, now that was smart."

"Remember, it is not just me knowing this, it is God placing the knowing into me."

"But for so many people to gravitate towards you Sandra? I mean it's a big world out there and to have so many in your area, be from the time of Jesus. How can you explain that?"

"Oprah, you are not asking questions of me, that I have not asked myself. And to be truthful, I don't know how to explain it to you." I looked into her face.

"The answer I give myself is why not? Why not me? Why not here? If the seed has been planted in me, if it is my purpose to know this information, well, I can only tell you what many wise people before me have discovered."

"And what is that?"

"God doesn't make mistakes. Accept the gift."

"Share the gift!"

"Exactly. I will celebrate that gift, Oprah. I may not have all the answers, but to everything, there is a purpose under God. I am believing that this amazing story that I have shared with you will too, in time, make its meaning known to us."

"Oprah, you have no idea of the many people who have come to me, saddened and lonely. Looking for answers. Some are in desperate life threatening situations. They have forgotten what an important light they are so spirit guides their way to someone like me who can reaffirm their strong light and offer them hope through a change of thought."

Oprah was quick to butt in with, "And a change of thought can produce an entirely different future."

"Right you are my friend. Well said!"

"Especially when the thought that you plant is that you are more than just this lifetime."

"Yeah, you are the combination of all your soul's lifetimes"

"We all know now after all our ego work that thinking positively and using the I AM words" I cut off her sentence and interjected, "Yeah, like I AM happy that you have come for a visit here with me Oprah!"

She smiled in recognition of this and echoed back to me. "Like I AM grateful to have been invited."

"And I am sorry."

"Please forgive me."

"Thank-you."

“I love you.”

“Yes.” And I switched over to my fake English accent to state. “And I love you too my dear!” We both smiled at one another.

“The two of us enlightened ladies are now laying down possibilities for more happiness and more gratitude in our lives because of the language we choose to speak.”

“Sandra, I certainly hope that more and more people will really hear what you are saying because it is what I have been doing my level best to promote this on my show.”

“And you have done such an excellent job of it Miss Moses, the Queen of the “I AM’ herself.”

“Yeah, Moses was all about the I Am wasn’t he?”

“Do ya think?” I answered back in a tone that made her smile. I took Oprah's foot and I gently placed it down. “Now, give me your other foot.” I commanded as I patted my lap with both of my hands.

“This feels amazing. My right foot is all tingly.”

“That’s just the blood and energy flow going through the foot. Your left foot will feel the same after I am done.”

“I am really beginning to relax” Oprah purred.

Chapter Fourteen

"I want to share with you a very important story."

"O.K., Sandra, go ahead" Oprah encouraged.

"Oprah, this is fascinating. It's about the time when God breathed Himself into me."

"Say What??? God breathed Himself into you? Now let me get this straight, you were visited by an angel, you prayed one Easter weekend and got the connection to the God voice. And then you found out that in a past lifetime you were the Roman Soldier?"

"And I was able to read past lives."

Oprah obligingly reiterated, "And you were able to read past lives?"

"Correct." I paused and I sighed.
"I'm doing my best to fill you in on all these past experiences so that you will understand why I am able to know the things I know."

Oprah gave me the nod to continue and I did.

"It was in February of 1994. Caring for my three small children was taking its toll on me. Not having had a holiday or a break away from the everyday had left me burnt out."

"I hear you Sandra. I can get so caught up in the giving that I too can get really low. Kind of low on energy and feeling slow."

"You always have a sure fire way of knowing when you REALLY need a break."

"How's that?"

"You keep on telling yourself that you don't need one." Oprah laughed out a little 'Humph.'

"You know how you know you need a break from taking care of the children?"

"How's that Sandra?"

"You don't want to leave them."

"Now that is funny."

"Funny? It's crazy! You continually make up excuses as to why they cannot live without you and you end up talking yourself out of holiday after holiday."

"So you were coming up with reasons why you didn't need a small mini-vacation?"

"Yes. And that is how I knew I had to take one!" We both smiled warmly at one another.

"Oh yeah. And what made it really an opportune time was that my in-laws were away and their house was gonna be empty. Empty and quiet."

"So if you had a great place to stay" I cut in and said, "At the right price." We both echoed at the same time, "Free!" and then laughed out loud.

"Why not go?"

I then told her, "Dave, my husband, agreed to manage our children, so, I was off! And Oprah, remember I was telling you how that voice from God was speaking to me now and then?"

"Yeah."

"Well, the voice came to me very strongly and told me to go and buy a tape recorder before I checked in at my free room and board. I complied. You know Oprah, it was so weird to be driving there and all of a sudden receive this knowing to stop arguing and questioning the voice. To just go and do what I was being directed to do. When I cease my arguing and just comply, the feeling of urgency leaves and I am calm again.

"Yeah, I can imagine those talking voices in your head can be a real bitch sometimes, eh Sandra?"

I was stunned by this and looked at Oprah with my mouth agog and saw that she was laughing!

"Are you making fun of me Oprah?" I grabbed at her big toe and began to squeeze it until she called uncle.

"Say uncle!" I urged her.

"Say uncle and it'll stop!"

"What in God's name are you grabbing on me that is causing so much pain?"

Ignoring her, I continued to squeeze. Then said, "Don't mess with a Reflexologist, Oprah. It can only mean pain!"

"O.k., O.K. Uncle, Uncle." She relinquished as I loosened my grip on her toe.

"I couldn't help myself Sandra. Honestly, I love to hear your stories. In fact, I'm loving every minute of this. But I just had to butt in and say that."

"Cause?" and I wasn't mad or anything that she said that. It was more of, well, I can take a ribbing.

"Cause it strikes me as funny. I don't have the same experiences as you and well, honestly, we are all so conditioned to believe that voices in your head can only mean one thing."

"That you are." And I sang "Coo-Coo."

"Well yeah. How do you know if the voices that you are hearing are, well, let's say from a sound source?"

"Oprah, that's a good question. I can only tell you that God's voice, or the voice of spirit for me, comes from inside as a gentle knowing. Not a strange voice. But a familiar voice. And it will not tell you to do anything that would harm yourself or another."

I paused and thought about whether or not there was something else to add. I wasn't getting anything so I nodded at Oprah in silence and she took this cue to meaning I was finished with my explanation.

"It just sounds kind of strange. You know, to hear you talk like that." And she motioned with her hands.

"I guess I was just letting my mouth spit out what my brain was thinking. No offence Sandra, really. Do go on!"

I squinted my eyes and looked at her while I surmised the sincerity of her apology.

"Should I go on? Maybe I needed that reality check? Yeah, my stories can sound strange if you have not had a similar experience. Or, if you have not as yet developed your psychic abilities.

Perhaps, she was feeling closer to me now and was indeed treating me like a good friend would treat another good friend, offering merciless teasing and copious reality and ego checks. Hmmmmm. I choose to believe the latter. Shrugging it off, I continued on with the story and the correct positioning of my fingers on her foot!

“I got to my destination and was instantly greeted with the sound that I had not heard in a very long time. Silence.”

Though still laughing somewhat after that last exchange, we both began to calm down and I had her ear once again.”

“I guess you don't get much of that when you have three kids!”

“No, Oprah, no you don't!”

“So I began to unpack my stuff and had an immediate craving for fish.”

“Fish?”

“Yeah, I know. When I have a time where I am being called by spirit to know it or hear it. Or share spirit with someone such as we are doing today, it seems as if I have a craving. No. A feeling to eat fish!”

Oprah muttered out a ‘Humph.’

“At the time I thought nothing of it. I had no idea what was ahead of me, so, I made myself a tuna fish sandwich. Afterwards, when I had finished my meal, which I ate in the silence of the house, I cleaned up and then immediately felt as if I had to lie down.”

Oprah’s eyes were closed now as she was really enjoying her foot rub! Once in a while a groan or deep sigh would come from her and I knew she was enjoying her foot treatment. I continued on…

“So, I lied down on the sofa and I must have dozed off. I am not sure how long I was asleep. I just remember waking up and hearing sounds coming from the front hall."

"I thought you said that you were all alone there?"

"Yes, I was. Only, I had a feeling that now I wasn't."

"That's creepy Sandra."

"Isn't it? Anyway, when I heard what I thought was the front door open. I felt an evil presence."

Oprah opened her eyes.

"Then, I thought I heard footsteps in the hall, as if perhaps my husband David had come in the front door. I felt the presence of our little dog, Tinkerbelle."

"You had a dog named Tinkerbelle?"

"Uh? Yeah. Why?"

"Well, nothing, it's just a cute name. Was it a small dog or a big dog?"

"Oprah." I paused and lifted my eyebrows up and then reiterated. "Tinkerbelle. Think about it for a minute." I paused and smiled as her face flushed.

"Small dog. Fairies. Peter Pan. I get it now. Go on. Go on! Was it really your dog and your husband coming in?"

"No, that is the strange part of it. Physically there was no one. However, I could have sworn I actually heard them as well as felt their presence with me." I shrugged my shoulders and said,
"Who knows Oprah, perhaps it was the energy present for what was about to happen. There were many sounds and sensations

going on. I kept asking myself, am I awake or am I asleep?"

"How did you know you weren't dreaming all this Sandra?"

"I knew I wasn't dreaming cause my eyes were open!"

"Oh!"

"My eyes were open and my body would not move! Oprah, I was frozen!"

Caught up in the story just as surely as if she were there in the room right along with me, Oprah's curiosity was peaking as she leaned forward. "You couldn't move? You couldn't move Sandra?"

"No. I was wigging out Oprah. Inside I am telling myself not to panic, however, I was panicking! I tried to calm myself by testing if indeed I was not in a dream. First I did a body check. One, eyes open. Check. Two, body moving. No check."

Oprah, raising her voice now, asked, "Well what the heck was going on?"

"That's just it, I didn't know! I was so frightened! Imagine awakening and not being able to move a muscle!"

"So what did you do" she questioned.

"Oprah, what could I do? I just laid there. Inside I am screaming what the heck is going on here? At the same time, I am doing a limb by limb assessment trying to get and arm or a leg to obey my command. Nothing. I looked around the room taking in all of the reality I could and then the strangest thing happened."

Oprah was leaning way forward in her chair at this point. Eyes wide open.

"All of a sudden, I felt two hands on the top of my head and then I heard someone taking in a deep breath that was blown into the top of my head!"

Oprah's mouth was open now, as she sat there dumbfounded. I whispered then to her.

"Oprah, I knew it to be the breath of God."

"Wow." Oprah whispered back to me, waiting for me to continue, but I did not. We both sat in the silence of the moment so that we could resonate with what it was I had just said. After a moment or two, I went on to further explain.

"Oprah, I could actually feel the warm breath on the top my head." I paused. Then told her, "And you know what happened then?"

She shook her head side to side in complete silence.

"Immediately I could move!" I sat straight up and I can remember thinking to myself, "What the heck was that?"

"How did you know that it was God, Sandra?"

"Well at the time, I knew it not to be of this world because it had a similar mystery to it like the time the angel visited me. But there is more than that Oprah."

And I took in a breath and stopped massaging her feet for second. "God placed the knowing into me that it was Him. Now, this was occurring over a period of about five minutes, so I am doing my best to recount for you what exactly did happen."

"So you're telling me that God breathed Himself into you and you were sitting there, what did you do next?"

"I remember sitting there processing all of my feelings and listening to the knowing inside of myself filing in all the information for me as to what was actually happening. I got really quiet, and yet I was still somewhat scared by it. I decided to call my husband."

"Were you able to get him on the phone?"

"Oh yeah, a Realtor is never far away from a phone."

"What did you tell him?"

"I immediately told him what had happened."

"What did he say when he heard that?" she asked.

"He listened without saying a word, Oprah. Total silence on the other end of the line until I had finished telling him everything. And then he did what most men would do in a situation such as this."

"And what was that, Sandra?"

"He assured me it was probably nothing." We both had a laugh.

"My husband, I am afraid, is like most men. He is not at all into the spirit."

Sympathies and mutual acknowledgment all around, I resumed treating Oprah's feet again.

"Oprah, the next day was even more wild."

"Hold up a minute. What did you do for the rest of the day?"
"I went out that evening to be with a friend whom I had met in abuse recovery classes."

"Did you tell her about this?"

"Yes. Oprah, it's like I told you earlier. When you have friends that are open to hearing you speak, knowing that you can channel spirit, they really just listen."

"So she believed you?"

"I have no reason to lie to her. Of course she believed me. It's great Oprah, to be able to have those kinds of friends who love you and accept you no matter what it is that comes out of your mouth!"

"I have a few of those myself, Sandra. I can relate to what you are saying. Continue on."

I paused for a moment to have another sip of my drink and then resumed work on Oprah's foot as well as my account of one of the most amazing times of my life!

Chapter Fifteen

"I remember waking up in the morning on the second day. It was lovely to hear the sound of absolute quiet greet me as I began my day. I had a leisurely breakfast and took my time getting dressed. My intention was to practice a little yoga."

"Did you?"

"Yes. I put on George Michaels "Faith" and Whitney Huston's "Body Guard."

"I thought that you were supposed to practice yoga to relaxing music?"

"If I was teaching a class, I would do just that. However, when I am on my own, I go nuts! I dance Oprah."

"You dance?"

"Yup, I dance and I sing and I also do yoga."

"All together?"

"Sometimes. I have some new yoga stretches and postures that have come through me lately that'll really open up those chakras!"

"Really? Will you show me some moves, Sandra?"

"Yeah. Maybe later I will. Anyways. Where was I?"

"You were dancing and doing yoga."

"Oh Right. I remember practicing for about an hour or so and then I can recall myself laying down on the floor of the living room for a rest. If I can remember correctly, I was laying in a position very similar, if not exact, to Christ on the cross. It was like I made a mental note to myself about the similarity and then I felt myself rising towards the ceiling. Oprah, I had an out-of-body experience."

"What do you mean?" she asked me.

"I mean I felt myself fall away from myself. Rise up! And then I don't remember what happened."

"You mean you fell asleep or something?"

"Well, I guess it was kind of like that" I answered slowly as I was trying to find the words to better describe what was transpiring. "It was more like I felt myself rise up to meet God. Then I came back."

"How did you know you had come back Sandra?"

"I knew that I had come back because once again, I was present in the room."

"So you were present once more and how were you feeling?"

"Euphoric"

"Well Lordy, Lordy Sandra. My oh my! So, you believe that you went up to God?"

"Well, yeah. I believe this because when I came to or woke up I could talk with God."

"You could talk with God? How was it different then than it is now or was before?"

"Great question, Oprah. When most of us pray to God, you must be still and wait for Him to answer. Whereas, in this case I was not being still any longer, I was up and moving around. His presence was immediate. It was in me, on me, all around me. I merely had to think a thought or a question and the answer to it was given to me immediately! And Oprah, I mean immediately."

I snapped my fingers to demonstrate.

"I would ask a question" I snapped my fingers again, "voila, answered."

"Uh, huh."

"I would just know the answer. God gave me the gift of Knowing. Knowing Him Oprah. And do you know what was amazing Oprah?"

She didn't answer me. She just shook her head from side to side indicating she didn't know the answer.

"I saw the room come alive." I paused for affect. I let the silence just hang there and finally continued on to tell her that, "Oprah, the answers to any of my questions to God were not only coming to me in knowings, but they were also in the room all around me."

"What was all around you, Sandra?" Oprah scrunched up her nose, looking to understand.

"The answers Oprah! The answers to my questions were all around me! It was like, the answer to any question that I had of God at any given moment was revealed to me by the things I would see, hear or smell. It was instantaneous and because it was happening at such an accelerated rate, I could communicate with God at lightning speed. Am I explaining this alright for you Oprah? Are you able to get a sense of this?"

"I think so, Sandra."

"I was in His world Oprah and He was letting me see Heaven. He was letting me 'Be' in Heaven. There was no separation between us. We were one."

I know what I was telling Oprah was profound. It was amazing. It was miraculous. It was my truth.

I mean it was a lot for me when it happened. I could not imagine how it was affecting her. I know that she has heard some amazing things in her day. I would guess this was also under the 'amazing' category!

"So, what did you do with this new ability?"

"I really didn't 'do' anything Oprah. I just allowed myself to 'Be' in it. It was like I was floating. Moving from moment to moment with such wide-eyed wonder and enthusiasm. I was in my own world with God and no one, and I mean it Oprah, no one could touch me."

"Meaning?"

"Meaning that no one could separate Myself from God. I was melded to Him and He to me."

"Wow!" Oprah just took this in as she sat there in silence. Her next question of me was.

"Was there anything of interest on the tape recorder Sandra?"

"That's the thing Oprah. I didn't listen to it for years afterwards. I was kind of rambling on. If you are interested, well, we could listen to it together sometime because, I really would like someone else's take on the matter."

Oprah was so quick to take me up on this that her mouth blurted out the words, “Whenever you can play that for me, I would love to hear it!”

“Good” I responded.

“I actually made two copies of the tape and sent one to James Redfield the author of The Celestine Prophecy. I was also going to mail one to Bobby McFarren cause he was Judas and to Steven Spielberg.”

“Steven Spielberg! Bobby McFarren is Judas?”

“Don’t try and make sense of it Oprah. I’ll know more about it when I get the chance to meet Him and together we can go over his lifetime and see if the Judas thing fits for him or not.”

“Like the Moses thing fits for me, Sandra?”

“Yeah.”

“Hmmmm. I am not sure of my connection to Steven Spielberg just yet. However, I do have a strong feeling, there is one. He had just released Schindler’s List. I think that could have something to do with it.”

“Hummm.”

“I did a lot of talking to Steven as if he was my best friend or something on that tape recorder I bought.” I began to laugh quietly to myself. Then I explained, “I don't know why I choose him to use as a confidant, but whatever the reason, when you listen to the tape, it's kind of funny.”

“Why is that?”

“It's cause I'm talking away to him as if I know him. He has absolutely no idea who I am and you wouldn't get that from listening to it."

"Maybe he was someone from one of your past lives?"

"Maybe, Oprah, maybe. Good observation. I had actually thought of that, however, I have as yet to do a reading on him."

"Why not?"

"I think it's because I am not meant to know this at this time."

"So, you're telling me there is some force that prevents you from doing this? Something that tells you whether or not you can receive information?"

"I am saying that when it is time for the information to be revealed to me, then it will be. I don't have to go and search for it with my mind."

"How do you search for information?"

"If you ask a question about someone or something, you can just leave it out there and when you are meant to know the answer, it will appear to you in some form."

"You just have to be awake to receive it, right Sandra?"

"You got it Oprah." I waved my hands back and forth and then said, "Look I am getting sidetracked, Oprah. I woke up from this out of body experience and I could speak with God."

"How long did this feeling or this ability to speak with God last Sandra?"

"Three weeks."

"Three weeks? That's an awful long time!" she exclaimed.

"Yes, yes it was. But oh Oprah, did I ever love it! I would wake up in the morning and open my eyes and say to myself 'It's still here!'… and then I would start my day. Everywhere I went it was with me and things moved so fast and efficiently. The world was alive! Oprah, it was alive all around me."

Oprah's eyes widened.

"I would have conversations with people and put into practice the teachings of The Celestine Prophecy. You remember? In order to get the meaning or message that is being brought to you."

"You send the person your energy. You send them love!"

"I did and it was amazing. I would get the information that they were there to give me quickly and then I was on my way. The Celestine Prophecy made it easier for me to handle the spirit world now that it was upon me."

Oprah stopped me, "What's that part now that you're working on my foot?"

"Sore eh?"

"Yeah, really sore."

"That's your hip."

"Oh, yeah, my left hip has been a little sore now that you're telling me this."

"Mine gets sore too" I sympathized. I continued to press upon it until it eased up.

"O.K., O.K., she urged me, Continue!"

"Honestly, Oprah it was such a kick being in this energy. I wasn't doing anything, or saying any extra prayers to make it stay. It had nothing to do with me. It was just there."

"So, you're really telling me that it was God who placed Himself into you? You had nothing to do with it?"

"Yes. But at the time, I wasn't trying too hard to analyze it, I was more interested in 'being' in it!"

"So, Sandra… did you ever once, while you there in this energy, think that you were God?"

"It was pretty hard not to."

"Why is that?"

"Because I was sending so much love to everyone I encountered as well as receiving it, that I did begin to wonder if when we are one with God, well does it mean that we are God for that time?"

"And what did you conclude, Sandra?"

"I guess I concluded that to be God, is to be one with everything."

"So?"
"So, to answer your question, Oprah, yes, for a time, I was knowing that I was God." Silence. Oprah was staring deep into my eyes.

"So how come you? How come God chose you to know Him, to see Him and to be able to be so close to you that you can actually sit there and tell me for a time of three weeks Sandra, that you were God?"

"It was because of my heart, Oprah. God told me he chose me

because of my heart."

Again I was met with silence. I could tell that she was really giving this her all. She reached over and poured herself another one of those cranberry drinks and sat there and thought about what we had just discussed.

"Did you keep a journal of this?"

"Yes. I did my best to document what was happening."
I paused and went quiet. I took a breath and then confessed to her right then and there.

"As ungrateful as this may sound Oprah, and I am embarrassed to have to confess this to you, after a three week period of being with God, just He and I together as one, I began to feel well, lonely."

"Why is that?" Oprah was quick to ask.

"Cause I couldn't share it with anyone."

"Help me understand Sandra" Oprah said, as she straightened herself in her chair.

"You're now telling me that you were in Heaven with God and you were feeling lonely? How can that be possible?"

"I know it doesn't really make sense, except, I would go to bed at night and not be able to share this with my husband because he just wasn't where I was."

"I think that I can understand that." She backed down somewhat and softened her tone. I think she was allowing what I had said to resonate with here.

"Yeah. I mean this was great. It was wild and truly fantastical.

Only I was taking a ride on a rollercoaster and after about the two hundredth go-around, I wanted to get off." I looked down at my lap and said in a soft voice, "My friends began looking at me with a blank stare that conveyed a 'What on earth are you talking about' look. Oprah, I was really on my own. After three weeks, I shrugged my shoulders and finished with, "I felt VERY lonely. It began to get me down." Pause.

"I can see why" Oprah empathized. She put her glass back on the table and continued on with, "You were having the adventure of a lifetime, of many lifetimes for that matter, and there was no one that you could share it with."

"Thanks for that Oprah. You know it may be hard for some people when they hear this, to understand why I was no longer up on cloud nine. The best way I can explain it to you so that you will truly understand, is…." I hesitated and then said, "It was the feeling Adam had in The Garden of Eden before God created Eve." And there was this pause.

I continued speaking… "You see the funny thing is Oprah, I do know how Adam felt because this experience allowed me to know."

"To know how it felt to be alone in the Garden of Eden?"

"Yes. To know how wonderful it is to know God and be in His amazing creation, and at the same time, longing to share it with someone. I believe that our journey here together has a great deal to do with sharing ourselves and our experiences with one another. It is one of the main reasons that I began to write about all my spiritual adventures. If I can share what it is that I know, perhaps you will be able to feel, not so alone yourself."

"So one of your intentions for writing is to share your stories of spirituality in hopes that others can identify with them?"

"Yes! Most certainly! I know for a fact if I had read about someone who had a similar experience to mine, I would have contacted them somehow, some way in order to compare stories."

"Perhaps, by doing this, you would have been able to better understand what was happening for you?" I smiled at this. Oprah got back to the story at hand.

"So, what did you do about the loneliness?"

"Well, I began to ask God if I could just be myself again."

"And did He answer you."

"Yes, He did. God always answers your prayers. I can still remember to this day, some sixteen years later how His energy left me."

I took a moment and had a drink. Moved around a bit and adjusted myself in the chair and prepared myself for the telling of the conclusion to my most coveted time with God.

Chapter Sixteen

"I was over visiting my neighbor who was having some marital, family problems. We were inside her garage as she was explaining some of the problems she faced. I offered to help her. Thinking in the back of my mind I have a direct line to the Big Guy himself right now. I will simply ask for a solution for this lady and get a direct answer. I turned to her and offered. "Well perhaps I can help you with that?" Then she turned to me and said angrily, 'Who do you think that you are? You're not Jesus Christ.' and Bam!" I used my hand to demonstrate an airplane plummeting towards the earth. At the same time, I made the sound of an airplane on its way down from the skies.

"Oprah, I instantaneously felt all that super-empowering God energy leave me. I had the sensation of falling Oprah, and it felt as if I had hit the concrete floor in that ladies garage with the full force of what felt like my entire body weight. It just left me. It just left me breathless and empty. I wanted to go home."

"And it was gone just like that?" Oprah asked. I reiterated to her in the same tone of voice.

"Just like that."

"So, what did you do next? Did you go home?"

"Oh I went home alright. And when I did, I walked into my house and lay down on the floor of the living room adjacent to the front hall. And now here is the really strange part that kind of ties it all together." I looked at Oprah and I had her full attention.

"What happened?"

"The same thing. I couldn't move."

"You couldn't move?"

"No. I was frozen. Just as I was before the energy came into me, here I was on the floor again and I could not move a muscle."

"So, was anyone home? What did you manage to do?"

"My daughter Caitlyn was home so I called to her and she came running immediately."

"What did you tell her?"

"I told her not to panic, but Mommy just couldn't move right now and could she run next door and get our neighbor?"

"And did she?"

"Yes."

"What were you thinking at the time, Sandra?"

"Well, again, I was scared. I didn't know what was happening to me. Thoughts were racing through my mind and when my neighbor came in with Caitlyn, I just told them to call 911."

"And did they?"

"Yup"

"Did they take you to the hospital?"

"Uh huh. Only on the way there, I slowly began to be able to move my body again. By the time the doctors saw me, I was back to myself again."

"So, things came back normal?"

"The doctor's questioned me as to whether I had been having a lot of stress in my life. Probably thought I was seeking attention. Either that or I needed a vacation."

"So, you went home?"

"Yes."

"Was it hard then for you to be back to your old self again? Were you still able to speak with God?"

"Oh yeah, I was glad to be back in the world that I knew. And for all intents and purposes Oprah, I felt just like my old self again.

And as for speaking to God, well, that too returned to normal. It wasn't as all as intense or as encompassing as before. It was as if something entered into me, and then it left."

"So, if I have got this straight, you were you again?"

"Good way of putting it. Yes. I was back to being me."

"Did you ever have it happen again?"

"Good question. Yes and No. Yes over the years I have had many bouts of intense God-energy fill me. I could write another book on the number of times!" I gave a little 'Uh' sound and continued on to tell her as I scrunched up my nose and did that puckering thing with my mouth, "And no, it has never been quite the same as that time."

"Why do you think that is, Sandra?"

"I'm not sure. I think that entire episode was like a glimpse. A taste of what it would be like to be Divine. To be with God. To live in The Garden of Eden."

"Hmmmm." Oprah was nodding her head up and down.

"But I do believe that there is something more though, Oprah."

"Like what?"

"Like why?"

"Why, what?"

"Why did God show me this?"

Oprah didn't have an answer so she sat there looking at me, most likely hoping I would come up with the answer. I did.

"I believe God showed me this, as well as taking me to the place of 'As it was in the Beginning' because the two are connected."

"I'm listening."

I took in a nice long deep breath as I allowed spirit to come forth and work with me on the answer.

"I am thinking that what happened to me in the story that I just told you about, will be happening to us all."

"Why is that?"

"Cause why have it happen to just me?"

"As far as you know, just you!"

"Yeah, right. As far as I know, I am the only one this has happened to. So, why did God show me this? There has to be meaning behind it."

"Because?"

"Because of the universal law states that everything happens for a reason."

"So you think that the reason this happened to you" Oprah asked a leading question.

"Is to tell people what to expect when the time comes for God to call us Home to Him. Home to Heaven."

"Are you saying that we all will go for a nap and wake up and not be able to move?"

"Yes, I guess I am." And I paused here, looked around, and took in a deep breath before I continued, "I guess I am telling you this so when it happens, people will not panic, but rather expect it."

"So you telling me you think that it's a rite of passage?"

"It has to be. Oprah. What happened to me was significant and I know this because I know my Bible. Where in the Bible do we first hear about God's breath? God breathing Himself into His first creation, Adam."

"Right. And throughout the Bible, we hear many times about the breath of God."

"When God's breath is involved, we understand that whatever action is taking place that it is to be deemed of God are we not?"

"I believe so."

"So, if God breathed into me, and I am being instructed by Him to write this book, this account of it… then there must be divine order taking place."

"Yes. Oprah. And I know this because it is different. It is

different than what other people are telling us about the end of days."

"Lots of people are sending out fearful predictions about what will happen."

"Yes they are. My prediction is more about how God will be calling us home to Him. How to seek Him out so that you may peacefully return to The Garden when He is ready to call you Home to Him."

"So, I may just lay me down to sleep like you did that day at your in-laws and next thing, find myself conscious, but rendered incapable of movement."

"If that was the sequence I went through, and there was a reason for it, then, yes, that is my conclusion."

"So don't panic when it happens to you. Because you have been warned that finding yourself in this predicament is a good thing and not a bad thing."

"Precisely. The next thing you know, you will feel God's breath upon you and "voila" you will be with Him in Heaven."

"So, Sandra. You believe what happened to you will eventually happen for many more of us?"

"Yes. Yes I do. I think that just about ties it all up. How is all of this sitting with you Oprah?"

"Hmmm." She uttered half lost in her thoughts.

"Can you come up with any other theory that would help to explain this?"

"No."

So, remembering what happened to you Sandra… well, you didn't die for one thing."

"No, in fact I think that alone gives us all hope."

"Why is that?"

"Because I lived. I did not have to die to go to heaven. I mean physically die."

"Right. But Sandra, at the same time, you became separated from all those around you."

"Yes I did. But Oprah, what would happen if this occurrence were to happen to more than just me?"

"You mean if many people woke up to find themselves conscious of the presence of God in themselves."

"And Oprah" I raised up my finger and pointed right at her as I said "And in others!"

"Then you wouldn't get so lonely because other people would be able to relate to you." I butted in right away with, "Exactly."

"Oh my Lord! Oh my Lord! I am just breaking out into those goose bumps all over my body Sandra!"

"It indicates what we are saying is true!"

"I am so glad that you have shared this with us all! I can't tell you how truly awesome I am feeling just hearing these words spoken to me."

"Well, it had taken years for me to find its meaning, Oprah. Years. The one thing I have learned about the world of spirit is that it takes time for all the pieces to fall into the right picture."

"You're pretty sure about this aren't you Sandra?"

"Yes. It makes the most sense to me. One thing more though Oprah."

"Yes, Sandra. Remember when I spoke of how it was that when I laid down on the couch for a rest at my in-laws and I heard noises and felt a presence of evil?"

"Yes. I remember you saying that."

"Did you not think that it was odd for me to feel a presence of evil at the same time God came to me?"

"Well yes, I did wonder about that. How could that have been?"

"That was my time of judgment."

"Your time of judgment?"

"Yes. I believe that what transpired at the time was this. When we come to God at the end of days, we will be judged. God on one side and the dark energy on the other."

"Satan, Sandra?"

"Yes Oprah, the big "S" word." I made a hand gesture that was spooky.

"I felt it was God who had called the dark energy to witness His claiming me as His own."

"So, you're telling me that this was the day you became God's?"

"I am believing this as well."

"Are you meaning that this too is how we all will be called Home to God? Is this how our judgment will take place?"

"It could be exactly like what happened to me. Look, Oprah, I am making my own theories based on my own experiences. That is it. It is all I can draw from. I simply have been lead to conclude how we will enter into the Kingdom of Heaven. Is that how it will happen exactly? I'm not sure because spirit is always moving and changing according to our thoughts. But I can't help but believe that I was shown God's master plan for our coming Home to Him. I believe it to date. You have the option to formulate your own theories about what you have just heard."

We both paused for a moment and smiled at each other. Oprah finally spoke.

"I think that you are one very special person Sandra and that what happened to you definitely was for a reason."

"Thanks Oprah."

"There still could be more reasons for this that will surface over time."

"True."

"But for now, I am fascinated with what it is that you have just shared with me. I will reserve my final judgment until later on. But first, I'm gonna have to use the ladies room again."

"Good timing because I'm just about finished your reflexology treatment."

We both got up and faced one another. Oprah smiled at me and said, "My feet feel marvelous! Tingly, but marvelous just the same."

“Well, take it easy, I usually tell my clients to rest for a couple of hours afterwards.”

“I think I'm in the right place for that!” she exclaimed as she took another look around.

“My, my… this is a beautiful place.”

“Yup, I just love it!”

“You don't own it, you rent it?”

“If the people who own it would sell it and if I had a way of raising the money, yes I would gladly own it. You know those shows that you have about making people's dreams come true?”

She nodded in acknowledgement.

“Well, this is mine. To be able to come and go as I please. I would most likely have to either winterize it or knock it down and build something. Either way, I shed many tears every year when my rental time is up and I have to leave.”

We just paused and stood gazing at the wondrous trees and the beautiful blue sky when Oprah countered with, “I just might have to shed a tear or two myself when I leave here today.”

“Well, if we don’t get time for a visit to the Garden, I might not get rid of you!” We both laughed.

Chapter Seventeen

It was time to go for a walk or a swim or something. I waited until Oprah came out of the washroom and into the family room.

“Hey Oprah, why don't we go for a walk on the beach and I will show you around?”

“That sounds wonderful, Sandra.”

“We'll walk and talk - O.K.?”

“O.K.” she agreed.

I had another thought. “We might as well get our swimsuits on now as opposed to later” I suggested and then if we decide we want to just jump in the lake, we will be dressed for it!”

“I like that idea Sandra. Just show me where to change!”

I directed her to a bedroom where Doug had placed her bags.

I gestured with my arms and pointed into the room as I spoke in an English accent, “You should find all that you need in here, Madame.”

Oprah mimicked my voice and in response said, “Why Thank-you my dear.” And raised up her arm and gave me the royal wave as she passed me by.

I went into my room and also began to change into my swimsuit. I went quiet and then thought to myself.

“If only I could tell you more Oprah. I have so many amazing stories to share! Oh I know it would take days to fill you in on all my mystical adventures, but what fun we would have talking about the world of the spirit! I know that you would love to hear about my spiritual birthday, or how God Himself came into me one day and attended a church service. The spirits of so many have spoken their stories to me. Heck, I even know the conversation that Satan had with Christ on the cross. I should know - it came through me! It is sooo cool that God is revealing so much information to us at this time." I smiled at myself in the mirror. "I guess that we are just ready to hear it now. After all, we are in the time of Revelation."

I shook my head and cautioned myself. "Watch what you tell her, Sand. Don't say too much. Remember you have had a long time to digest this. Oprah is just hearing a lot of in now. It could take awhile for the two of us to feel comfortable enough with one another before I would be able to tell her things that at this point and time, would do nothing more than scare her or alienate her to the point where she would not be able to hear me."

"Hmmmm. Go slowly Sand. Just let spirit guide you and don't doubt yourself! All is good!" I looked at myself in the mirror again and adjusted my bathing suit, my hair and put on my shirt, sunglasses and hat.

"For years I have believed that I was pregnant with the word of God. That the Mother Mary energy was inside of me as well." And I turned sideways, took in a rather large deep breath and let my belly relax. It looked as if I were nine months pregnant. How can this still be here? God's message, in me, just waiting to be born. Ugh! I feel so big! Get this energy out of me Lord!

The energy in me is the energy of God and all it seeks is to find expression. To plant seeds of change into the minds of God's children is what this book of mine is all about. Writing this book and revealing all that I know should be enough to get this belly off of me already!" I then straightened up and sucked my gut back in. "Better!" and with that, I turned and went out into the family area where Oprah was standing her back to me, observing the water from the front window.

I thought to myself again, "I think it's going pretty well. She appears to actually be having a good time! Good food, great stories. Not to mention a reflexology treatment to boot! Yeah, she's having fun. I was assuring myself. After all, Oprah likes all this stuff! Almost as much as I do! She has been just great coming all the way up here. I hope that she does not go home, empty-handed. I really want to get her into the Garden and see what happens. Heck, I'm even excited to witness what transpires this day. Will God come to visit Oprah in my Garden? Will she actually hear Him as I do?"

I startled Oprah as she was lost in thought.

"Nice bathing suit Oprah! My favorite colors, green and purple!"

"Oh Sandra, I didn't hear you. I was lost in thought just staring out at the beach."

I walked up beside her and said, "It's pretty awesome being so close to the water. I just love watching the waves and people walking by."

Oprah looked at me and smiled. "I just am having such a good time with you here today Sandra. I am actually able to relax and just forget about everything!"

"I'm sorry that you were unable to bring your dogs this time. They would have had so much fun running on the beach and playing in the water."

"Don't I know it!"

"Come on. Let's head down there and we can go for a walk!"

Chapter Eighteen

In a matter of minutes, towels in hand. We were stepping out the door and onto the beach.

It was late afternoon, around four. The sun had passed overhead and it was reflecting like sparkling diamonds upon the lake.

"Oh my God, Sandra! Just look at this!"

"I am one lucky duck Oprah. I mean I know it is no California Coast line, but it is home for me!" The wind was warm and blowing Oprah's hair in all directions. She put down her beach bag and towel and put on her scarf.

"Sandra, shall we go for a walk on this lovely beach before we swim?"

"Great idea" I answered.

We began to make our way to the shoreline.

"This is so relaxing and so beautiful! No wonder you love it here so much."

"It is the best place. See that cottage over there?" I pointed to the one on our left, then continued to explain.

"That is the cottage my grandparents owned when I was a kid."

Oprah looked and asked, "Was it always like that?"

"No, they renovated it after they bought it from us in 1965."

"It's cute." Oprah offered.

"Yeah. It used be smaller and the bedrooms all lined up at the front so that you could lie in bed at night and listen to the waves hitting up on the shore. I feel asleep many a night listening to that sound and awoke many a morning listening to the calm of the lake before the wind would pick up again and send the waves rolling up onto the shore once more. And see this creek up here?" I motioned to Oprah.

"Oh yes" she said as we walked up towards the mouth of it.

"This is where I would come to catch frogs and butterflies with a homemade net my grandmother concocted out of a hanger and an old pair of her nylon stockings." We both smiled and she asked me.

"Did you ever catch anything?"

"Oh yeah. Once in a while I would catch a butterfly or two."

"Any frogs?"

"Nope. I left that to my brother. He was the one that got right in there in the mud and hunted them out!"

"Sounds like a fun time Sandra."

"Yup. It was great. I would love to go swimming right about here." And the two of us walked over to the spot. We both stared out into the lake.

"I would come and swim for hours and hours. As long as an adult would watch me for is the amount of time I would stay in the water."

"You wouldn't get all pruned up?"

"Oprah, at the time I was a kid. So the answer is "Who cares?" I was having fun and it was all that mattered to me. I swear I could swim for hours upon end. Come on! Let's walk down this way for awhile."

We began to walk southwards. There was silence and we both drank it in. We remained quiet for some time, listening to the waves and warming our faces in the sun. As we strolled along I shared with Oprah stories about various cottages along the way.

"This is a cottage that we used to rent before we rented the one that we are at currently."

"Oh it's nice too. How long were you renting that one?"

"I'd say about nine years or so."

"Why did you leave?"

"The people that we rented from were no longer interested in renting so we had to find a new one to rent."

"Well, weren't you emotionally attached to this one?"

"Hell, yeah! It was so hard not to be able to continue renting the same cottage that our children had grown up believing was their cottage."

"I can imagine."

"Yeah, anyway, as the years pass, we have come to love this other cottage just as much! However, there is a piece of this place that will always live on in my heart."

Oprah smiled and again we walked up the beach in silence. Every once a while I would point out friends of ours cottages and give her some local history. Some history more colorful that others. It was not until we had gone a quarter mile when Oprah began to speak about our past hours together.

"Sandra, there is something I would like to get off my mind."

"Oh, O.K. what is it?"

"Well my mind has been going over all the stories that you have shared with me. I can't shake the feeling that there has to be something more."

"Such as?"

"Such as, God has come to you on more than several occasions. You have had many encounters with the world of spirit. I know that there most likely are more stories that you have not as yet shared."

I looked up from watching for shells on the beach and smiled broadly at her.

"Yes. There are more."

"So, you have shared that you are The Roman Soldier and in one of your past lives. Are there any other past lives that you have had that you can share with me?"

I was smiling to myself because this is the very window I was hoping spirit would open up for me so that I could share more of myself with Oprah. I paused and waited so that spirit could begin to work through me.

"Oprah, over the past twenty years or so, I have learned a lot about our past lives. It seems that most of us have anywhere between seven or eight past lives up to three hundred!"

"Really, that many?"

"Yes. So if you average it out, most people will have had about thirty past lives."

"Wow." Oprah responded with raised eye brows. Then asked "So how is it that you can figure out how many past lives you have lived?"

"Great question. Tough answer. I know of a number of ways to determine that. Some people are able to know through their psychic abilities. Some people must consult others. And some people just have a strong feeling that they were in another time. To them I say, do not doubt yourself. Believe it!"

"Alright."

"I found out how many past lives that I have lived through my own channeling and also from consulting other seers."

"So, how many past lives have you had then Sandra?"

"I believe around eight hundred!"

Oprah turned sharply and echoed back at me

"Eight hundred!"

I let out a "Whaww" sound shaking my head as if I had been shocked.

Oprah grabbed my arm and stopped me from walking. Staring at me she said, "I can't believe it! That many!"

"I was blown away too when I heard that from a great psychic I visited in Fort Erie. I knew I was an old soul. I just didn't know how many times I had been reincarnating."

"Wow." I think Oprah was trying her best to integrate what I had just shared with her. Now for the big bomb!

“Oprah, I journal and have been journaling most of my life. I started keeping a diary when I was in grade seven!”

“Grade seven? Good for you Sandra.”

“So, over the past years, when God speaks to me, he/she will tell me more and more about myself as we become more entwined.”

“Gottcha.”

“So, about five years ago…” as I reached up and grabbed Oprah’s arms, I said to her “God began to reveal to me that I was the angel who fell to earth as Eve.”

Oprah let go of my arms now and stared at me in disbelief. Then she said. “God told you that you are Eve.” It was a statement, not a question.

“Yes. And I have had many a seer and many a psychic confirm that too me time and again. But Oprah, they were only confirming what God Himself had told me. That is what makes it so cool!”

“I’ll say that it’s cool.” We began to do the walk and talk thing again, only we were not doing a lot of talking. Just walking and thinking.

Finally I said, “Oprah, it’s just like I told you. When you find out that you were somebody really cool in a past life, it takes awhile to integrate the information.”

Still no word from Oprah.

“Look, Oprah. It has taken me some time with this one too.”

"But what does it mean then, Sandra?"

"I don't follow you."

"Well, that your soul is one of the first souls on earth. Sandra the only other soul older than you is Adam!"

I smiled at her and nodded my head in agreement as I said.

"Yes, you are right."

Oprah stopped once again, faced me and said "So, what's the meaning?"

"You mean, why is it so great?"

"Well if I am Moses and God has entrusted me to bring in awareness. To help His children discover a new earth or as you say Sandra, and new way to be on the land. What are you to do? I mean, seeing that you are Eve."

Oprah shook her head a couple of times and brought her hand up to her forehead and began to rub her third eye area as if it were asleep and this action would awaken it to provide some kind of insight as to how to digest this most recent of disclosures.

"I am to guide all my children Home."

Silence ensued. I looked deep into Oprah's eyes and smiled. We both stood there on the beach, the wind blowing our wraparounds gently up against our legs. The sun was making its way over towards the western horizon.

"Sandra, my mind is absolutely spinning. I am doing my best to just allow all the information that you have given me to sink in."

We smiled at one another. I laughed a little and offered up to her.

"I know. Give it some time. I mean when you begin to put all the puzzle pieces together. They do make sense."

"Such as?"

"Such as I was visited by an angel. I have powerful psychic abilities. I know who people were in past life times. I can speak to souls that have crossed over. I talk to God. The one gentleman I was telling you about, he put it like this. I have had so many lifetimes of gathering knowledge - I just want to share it with the world."

"You're everybody's Mom Sandra. That's who you are. You're EVERYBODY'S MOM! We all came from you and Adam!"

"We all came from God, Oprah. I just was the first soul to inhabit a physical female body."

"Still. You're old!" she teased me.

"Yeah. I get it. I could use some of you favorite facial cream!" Oprah ignoring my joke continued talking.

"So, Sandra. Do you remember being in the Garden? Oh My God!" and she stopped and placed her hand over her mouth and just stared at me. It took her a moment as she then gasped out "Sandra, no wonder you invited me to your Garden. Oh. My. God! Your Garden. Eve's Garden. I mean it's like, really THEE GARDEN."

"Well, it is my garden. I believe people can build their own." Oprah was having none of it and butted right in, "No. No. It's really the garden. It has to be Sandra. It has to be if you're Eve.

I thought for a moment. Hmmm. Yeah, maybe she is right about this. It's not that I haven't ever thought about it that way before. It's just. It's just that I have a habit of downplaying my importance. My world of spirit is all so normal to me. I do not see myself as someone special. I simply see myself as just being like everyone else. I paused and let out a 'Humph.' I continued thinking and allowed what Oprah said to be true. I responded with.

"Well, truly it is a mystical and magical place for me. For in my Garden, God does come and go. I sing to Him and He speaks to me. I feel I am one with Him while I spend time in His presence. It's just that He told me everyone can have their own gardens. So, naturally, I did not conclude mine was special."

"Well obviously, I am here to enlighten you my friend!" We both smiled at that.

Chapter Nineteen

Just as I was about to speak, a hawk flew down very low in front of us and a feather fell. I let out a "Wow!"

"See, Oprah, a hawk feather!" and I raced over to it, bent down, picked it up and walked back over to Oprah with my newly found treasure in my hands.

"Yeah, I see it." I showed it to her and we examined it together. I thought of something great to tell her.

"There is a book that I read called 'Animal Speak' written by Ted Andrews. It's my spiritual bible. His writings give meaning to the world around us. Oprah, when I am up here for my holidays I find myself consulting it several times daily."

"How so" Oprah looked inquisitive.

"In this book are the meanings, the spiritual meanings behind birds, animals and insects. Oprah, let's say that I am sitting here on the patio and a blue jay flies by and rests upon a branch in front of me. This event sends to me a signal that the universe, God, spirit, wants to relay a message to me. I immediately consult the book and it explains not only the characteristics and habits of the bird, but also what spiritual message is being sent to me."

"Really?"

"Yes really." I was starting to speak faster again because I was spilling over with excitement about what I was telling her.

"Oprah, when we get back to the cottage, I will let you read through the book and we will look up together the meaning of Hawk."

"You mean because a hawk flew by us and dropped us a feather, that event has a spiritual meaning to it?"

"Right. It's how spirit talks to us. Oprah, it goes farther than that. Oprah, have you ever heard of a man named Ted Andrews?"

"I'm not sure. He sounds familiar."

"Oprah, I read 'Animal Speaks' like my Bible. Oprah, he teaches us how to talk, actually communicate with the world of nature and spirit in nature."

"Really Sandra. It sounds like you're quite a fan on this Ted Andrews."

"That would be an understatement. If we all are able to read Ted Andrews book and begin to accept the meanings that are written within as an absolute, then we will be able to develop a commonly shared language that once accepted, will be the beginning of a new language. The language of the spirit."

"What you are saying to me is that this fellow Ted Andrews…"

"Right."

"…Has written what the spiritual world is saying to us when we see a Goldfinch or a Cardinal for instance."

"Yes. And animals also."

"O.K. And that this meaning if accepted as truth by everybody will serve as a way of actually being able to speak with nature?"

"It'll be like learning French or Spanish. Only with this book, we can talk to the animals!"

"Like Doctor Doolittle?"

"Yes! Yes! Yes! Oprah, just think what this means. This gives words to animals, birds and insects that before could not communicate with us because there was no understandable language. Now, if we agree to read this book and accept it as a truthful way of communicating with Nature, then we could be present with God's meaning."

"You're saying we could then know what God was saying to us?"

"Yes. Oprah, I believe it is how past civilizations spoke with spirit. Now, we can too! Oprah, I have been using this for years up here and in most, if not all of my work. It is absolutely dead on with its meanings."

"Really?" she replied.

"I believe, we will eventually be teaching our children with this in our schools, right alongside of our alphabet."

"I can see the wisdom in this, Sandra."

"Oprah, I don't think that the idea of this is that far-fetched either. I actually believe that it is a return to understanding the meaning behind nature that our ancestor Native American Indians practiced and tried to pass onto us through their drawings and etchings."

"A 'return to the land' so to speak, Sandra?"

"A New Earth Oprah!"

"Touché!"

"You got it. For example, Hawk is a bird that represents Messenger. Isn't that what today is all about Oprah? It's me giving you a message that you may or may not choose to pass onto others.

The look of amazement on her face was obvious.

“Oh my God, Sandra. Is that what this means?”

“According to Ted it does. Oprah, see how easy it is to learn just what nature and God are trying to convey to us? It makes it like a whole new language that we all can learn and when we do, it’ll make being in the moment that much more ‘Ah Hah!’ because it will no longer be people saying to one another, ‘What do you think that this means?’ Oprah, we will actually know!” I was so proud of myself for getting this message to Oprah.

“Sandra, have you met this Ted Andrews?”

“He is on my list of people that I am going to meet someday Oprah. I want to thank him for giving us this gift of communication with God and nature.”

“I could have him on my show” Oprah offered.

“I bet he'd come too! Man, this is so exciting. I handed over the feather to Oprah. I know that this is a rare feather to have and I want you to have it to remember our day and the messages that you are receiving here.”

“I think that I have received many messages and I just need some time to write them all down before I forget them!”

“You'll remember, just tell yourself you will and, you will.”

“Let's turn around and head back to the cottage and have our swim.”

We turned and we continued to talk.

Chapter Twenty

“Look Oprah, we are just about home now. Let's have our swim and then go up for dinner.”

The two of us removed our hats and sunglasses then placed them carefully upon our towels that had been left on the beach in front of our cottage.

“Oh I hope that the water is warm, Sandra.”

“Oh, it’s been really lovely these past few weeks Oprah. I think you’ll be surprised.

Oprah approached the water. She moved cautiously over the small stones and right up to where the water meets the shore.

“Just take your time and let your body adjust to the temperature” I cautioned.

Oprah stuck her foot into the water. I waited for the judgment.

“Ohhhhh. It’s really warm.”

“I told you. Come on, just follow me.” We both began to wade up to our waists.

“Just fall back into it!” I urged her.

“I'm just taking my time.” Oprah replied slowly stating her sentence.

Just then, I began to get that funny feeling I get when spirit is entering into me. It came upon me like a heavy knowing and as I began to speak, I knew it was not me, but spirit. I began to channel to Oprah what spirit was wanting us to know.

“Hey Oprah, I summoned as I began to speak slowly and purposefully.

“Do you know why Barack Obama is going to become President?” Oprah scrunched up her nose at me and then said, “Because he is the best man for the job.” This was a statement.

“Yup, but there is another reason” I told her as I was swimming around, doing the breast stoke so that I could swim and talk at the same time.

“What's that?” she asked.

“Well” and I took my time telling her this, “It has to do with you.”

“Why, because I have publically endorsed him?”

“Well, it really has a lot to do with you and who it is that the two of you once were in a past lifetime.”

Oprah’s eyes widened.

“So Sandra, go on. You’re picking up on another past lifetime of mine Sandra? What is it?”

“That you and Barack Obama once lived as King and Queen in Africa.”

Her eyes lit up!

“Really?” she was nodding her head up and down.

“Really.”

“NO!”

"Yup. Not only did the two of you rule over the land successfully, but you both accomplished a great many things."

"So you're saying that Obama will win because of that past relationship?"

"I am not saying that he will win, I am saying that he will become President. It is history repeating itself. You both ruled harmoniously then and you will again."

"So the energy that existed between us before, in another lifetime is also present between us again?"

"Yes. Oprah I have been made aware by spirit that you were once a queen. I just didn't know until now where and with whom."

I paused and waited again for spirit to speak. It didn't take long.

"America will have its first Queen in you."

"Say what?" Oprah was stymied.

"I am saying that I can see visions of your coronation as the first royalty of America."

I paused and let Oprah receive this. After a few seconds of silence I assured her.

"And it makes perfect sense. You're spirit Oprah" I stood up in the water and faced her. I took her hands in mine as I continued to explain, which is Moses' spirit. Which is the spirit of God. It is THAT spirit being acknowledged.

"Oprah, you are to be crowned America's first royal Queen."

She stood there and stared into my eyes conveying disbelief. Finally after what seemed like a long time she spoke to me.

"Oh Sandra! How can you make such outrageous claims?"

I smiled at her, allowing the moments of silence to lengthen, knowing that she was needing these precious seconds to integrate this wonderful message from God and spirit.

"Think about it Oprah. You have been leading Americans on the road to self enlightenment, to their spirit for twenty-five years or so!" Here I let out a "Wah Whoooo!" as I got her to look up at me in disbelief of what she was hearing.

I went on to tell her, "You have ruled over day time television capturing all our hearts! Given hope to so many Oprah. So, so many." I paused. Then spoke in a more quiet voice.

"You're America's Queen Oprah. Only you just have had it hidden from you until now. In fact, I didn't even know this until right now either. I am just as filled with awe."

Oprah was looking down into the water. Somewhat humbled upon hearing spirit now speaking through me. I continued on in spite of her obvious embarrassment.

"Seriously Oprah, just listen and I know that your mind is thinking "down ego, down!" We both laughed at that!

Oprah let go of my hands and splashed me! We both began to splash at one another in the water.

"O.K. if you don't believe what it is that I am saying, then do your homework."

"Do my homework?"

"Yes, when you get back home, start to research as much as you can about past African and even Egyptian Queens."

“Egyptian? I thought you just said African?”

“I did, but there may be more than one life time that you and Barack have been affiliated.”

“You’re serious, aren't you girlfriend?”

“I have never been so serious.” I took up her hands in mine once more.

“Oprah, America needs to step up now and take her place in history along with the great countries of Europe.” I paused again and looking straight into her eyes I spoke the words, “Your country needs you to do this.”

I was feeling the seriousness of the energy that was coming through me. I continued to explain to her.

“American needs to give itself permission to be worthy of greatness. Your county has helped so many. Your country, Oprah, (and I have many tingles running through my body as I say this) has earned her stripes and stars. American has earned her Queen!”

We both stood there in wide-eyed wonderment as the spirit began to enter us both.

Oprah and I both now had goose bumps all over our bodies. I exclaimed enthusiastically, “Can you feel that???”

“I can Sandra, I can. Oh my God! I am just breaking out in goose bumps!”

“A sign that what is being spoken is a truth.”

“Oh my God. Sandra. I feel so light. I can hardly catch my breath.”

I stood there with her, tingling all over. Spirit came through me in a vision.

“Oprah, I am getting a vision of your ordination.”

“What? What is it that you’re seeing Sandra?”

“I can see bright colors. Oranges and browns. Feathers. Big plumes of orange and brown feathers on a head dress. I can see you walking down a long isle with a majestic robe trailing behind you.”

“Where is it being held, Sandra?” Oprah asked me excitedly.

“I’m not sure.” I answered slowly. Still waiting to receive more information from spirit.

“I keep seeing England because that is where we recognize the coronations of Kings and Queens. I also see quite an African influence there. So, the picture that I get is yet to be clear on that. Probably it'll have a lot to do with what America decides.”

“What do you mean?”

“I mean it will depend upon where America decides it would like to hold your coronation, Oprah.”

“As yet, no one has given themselves the authority to act on this.” I spoke these words slowly as I was receiving them from spirit though voice and pictures. I then told Oprah.

“I am getting the message that God Himself, would like to see this happen because your coronation, will unite the country of America, as it has never united under one banner before. Think about it Oprah, it wouldn't matter whether you were a Democrat or Republican, everyone can all agree on you.”

Oprah and I began to cry as the two of us hugged one another in the water. Just then I felt spirit move in me so strongly as I relinquished the grip we had on one another and went very still. I calmed myself and Oprah gave me a look that said, '"Hey why has the party suddenly stopped?"

I held my hand up to my mouth and made a sign for her to be quiet. Spirit took a hold of me now and I reached into the water and I pulled up my wet hand and I said to her then and there, "Oprah, be still now and receive the Holy Spirit of God. I too was crying with the beauty and the wonderment of the moment. Oprah watched me, fixed in time as I spoke to her.

"Kneel down Oprah." And there in the shallow water on the edges of Lake Huron, Oprah Winfrey knelt down onto one knee. I felt my hand reach into the water and come up to mark the sign of the cross onto Oprah's forehead as I heard myself say. "I now baptize you as America's first and lawful Queen in the name of God the Father, Christ the Son and in the name of God's Holy Spirit. May the love and wisdom of God guide you now and throughout the remainder of your days. May His Holy Spirit reside within you and keep you safe. Always. Arise, Queen Oprah."

I held out both my hands to her and she took them and rose slowly to her feet. We embraced one another in silence. We then hugged for what seemed like such a very long time. After a few moments we broke our embrace and I whispered to her, "Did you feel that?"

"Yes, I most certainly did Sandra."

"That was God's spirit upon us."

"It felt so warm, so light."

"Yes. And I can see that you also got the tingles" I pointed to her arms.

“Yes, I most certainly got the tingles that time. Sandra, I, I don’t know what to say?”

“Say nothing” I smiled lovingly at her. I could tell that she was somewhat disorientated. Like she was in shock. Unable to decide what to do next. So, I gently ushered her out of the water and onto the shore where she sat down immediately upon our towels. I held one out for her and then proceeded to wrap it around her shoulders. I then crouched down beside her and said softly. “That was a lot, eh?”

“Yes. Yes I am telling you that it was a lot to take in.”

“Yeah, I know. When you get the really important messages from spirit, it can leave you feeling like this. Not to worry, Oprah. Look, take your time here. There is no hurry to get up and do anything.

Oprah was silent. After a moment she said, “Sandra, do you mind if I just sit down here by myself for a while?”

“Not at all. I'll go up and get dinner started. You just take your time and I will give you a shout when it's ready.”

She smiled a smile of gratitude and as I was walking back up to the cottage I turned and yelled at her.

“Hey Oprah, it's not really that big of a leap for you! After all, you already got the money!”

I turned and laughed to myself at that one and headed up to make dinner.

Chapter Twenty-One

A good half an hour went by before I could detect any signs of life from Oprah's direction.

I was standing at the BBQ grilling our salmon steaks as Oprah made her way slowly up from the beach.
"You O.K?"

Lost in thought, she looked up at me. "Uh? Oh yeah, It smells just wonderful! Sandra, I'm just going to change into my clothes."

"Great, dinner is up so as soon as you're ready."

"I'll just be a minute."

"White wine with that?"

"That would be great."

I placed all the vegetables and salmon on the table right beside the salad. Poured the wine and just as I had finished, Oprah appeared. She came down the steps and sat at the table. We smiled, I offered to say the blessing.

"Thank-you Lord for your awareness and blessings on this day. We ask that you continue to direct our conversation and that you bless this food before us. In Jesus' name, Amen."

"It looks just fabulous Sandra."

"Thanks Oprah. Remember I told you whenever I am in the spirit and there is an important exchange of God's energy between two people that I seem to desire fish. Weird eh?"

"Why is that I wonder, Sandra" Oprah asked.

“I think that it has something to do with the energy of fish. After all, isn't the universal meaning behind the sign of the fish means Jesus?”

“Yes, it is.”

I shrugged my shoulders and casually said, “Humph, I guess that's the reason. It just affirms God's work is being done through us today.”

“I never thought of it that way.”

I paused and passed the salad to Oprah. “Thanks” she said and helped herself.

“Sandra.” she looked up at me.

“Uh huh.”

“By the way, my feet still feel wonderful!”

“I’m glad Oprah. You'll sleep like a baby tonight!”

“Oh, I guess that means that I'm staying overnight eh?”

“Well, it's almost nine o'clock and I have a small bonfire set at the beach. I was hoping that if things went well and you were to stay that you might enjoy a beautiful Lake Huron sunset and a fire out under the stars!”

“You make it sound just like heaven Sandra.”

“It is heaven Oprah, it's my heaven.” I then turned towards the Garden and motioned with my head towards it and said, “Besides, you still have not as yet had a chance to enter into the Garden.”

"I am so looking forward to that experience. Sandra, if tomorrow is anything like it was today, I'm going to need a good night's rest!"

I didn't have the heart to tell her that the bed she was going to sleep in, like all the other beds in this cottage were, well somewhat of a challenge. I decided to give my guest the master suite because it was the best bed out of the three.

"I think that you should give Gayle a quick call and tell her about the change in plans."

"I was just going to do that. What time do you think that I will be leaving tomorrow Sandra?"

"Well, Oprah, I guess that it depends on how long it is that you would be spending with God in the Garden."

"Right, I think that I'll just tell her that I will be in touch with her tomorrow."

"Good idea!"

While Oprah excused herself to call Gayle, I made short work of clearing the table and doing up the dishes. Oprah came back and when I saw that she had finished making her phone call, I told her to dress warmly.

"Sweaters, shoes and socks if you have them Oprah!"

"It gets that cold at night?"

"Yup. Once we light the fire it'll warm us up, but the sand after dark can get really cold. So, dress warmly."

We made our way down to the beach once again and we both took along a chair to sit on. I managed to light the fire with only one match and we cozied-up together and looked out over the lake.

“This is simply beautiful Sandra. I can't get over the colors in the sky!”

“Well Oprah, Lake Huron sunsets are famous. It is a different picture every night!”

“I wish that I had thought to bring my camera!”

“That's funny coming from you.”

“Why is that?”

“Well, your whole life it seems is in front of a camera. Are you not enjoying being away from them?”

“That's true.” Oprah looked at me and smiled. She quietly said, "So you’re telling me to just be in this moment. Aren't you?”

“Hey, we are all just creatures of habit. Being in the present is about seeing yourself as you are and then allowing it to be O.K.”

“I get it Sandra.”

“Let’s just take in a few deep breaths and really just be here in all this beautiful energy. God has made this particular sunset just for you and me Oprah. Let's enjoy it because there will never again be another one just like it.”

We sat in comfortable silence for quite awhile. I could tell that Oprah was happy and oh so pleased with our day. I was too. I know that I had told her a lot and there was much to remember. I am only praying that she will be open for our day together tomorrow and God will show up!

The rest of the evening we chatted about our personal lives. Our families, our friends and the people that we have met that had made the biggest impact upon our lives. We wondered how many lifetimes there have been where we were together and wondered who it is that we were to each other. After a while, all the stars had come out and you could even see the Milky Way.

Eventually, the blazing fire had burned down low and coals, just perfect for roasting marshmallows remained. We giggled, sang some campfire songs and ate marshmallows to our hearts content.

"I think I have had enough sugar Sandra" Oprah sighed as she placed the last of the marshmallows into her mouth (the last one without even roasting it!)

"Oh, I think you and I are getting a sugar high, Oprah!"

"I second that."

"We both will probably fall into bed in a diabetic coma I am sure."

"This is one great night Sandra. I am stuffed!" she said while patting her tummy.

"Me too!" I echoed.

"Why don't we get a move on Sandra? I think I hear my bed calling my name!"

After we were done cleaning up and put out the fire, we both dragged our bodies back up to the cottage.

"You may have already noticed this, Oprah…" I began as I held the cottage door open for her. "But the funny thing about our cottage is that the walls don't reach all the way up to the ceiling."

"Yeah, I did make a mental note of that Sandra and was going to ask you why that was?"

"I don't have a clue. But it was the same in my grandparent's cottage. It offers you no privacy whatsoever! Why you can hear everything any one says or does as if you were lying right there beside them!"

"So if you're up here with friends?"

"I tell them right away, No fooling around, because we can hear you - no matter how quiet you think that you're being!" Oprah and I chuckled to one another at that.

"So my question for you my dear is, you don't snore do you?" We both laughed like school girls at a pajama party.

After we had taken turns using the washroom and we safely tucked into our respective sleeping quarters I called out to Oprah.

"You know what we always do up here before we go to sleep?"

"No, what?"

"Well, it's not much fun cause there is just the two of us, but we do that good night thing that they do on the Walton's. You know, when they say good night to each other."

"I remember."

Then I called out in the Walton manner.

"Goodnight Your Majesty." And she echoed back to me, "Goodnight Sandra. I had a pleasant "Eve" ning!" I smiled to myself at this and within about five minutes we were both sound asleep.

Chapter Twenty-Two

It was a beautiful, day when I awoke. I looked out of my window and I saw the sun coming up just over the tree tops. The noise coming from the lake was at minimal and I could instinctively tell that the water was calm. I immediately jumped up and put on my yoga outfit and after visiting the ladies room, I went to sit outside and wait for my honored guest to arise.

I looked out over the property and began to just take in some nice big breaths. I came into the moment and was able to bring into my reality that Oprah, thee Oprah Winfrey was at my cottage. This was just awesome! I am the luckiest person in the world to be able to spend this time with her and to have the privilege of sharing my work with her in an environment where there are so little distractions. God has truly blessed me and I am so grateful to be able to take in the meaning of this encounter. I know now that not only is Oprah here to listen to my work and to be able to go into the Garden, but also to receive the knowing of God's plan for her.

I laughed to myself.

I didn't even know until yesterday if I was to even tell her all that. I was thinking that when I first appeared on her show that I would surprise her and greet her with a curtsey. She would wonder what I was trying to tell her by that action. It turns out that God's plan is to tell her now. Hummmm. Maybe because God is wanting to have this information so that she could prepare for what changes lay ahead for her?

Oh well, I am only the messenger. The meaning will be made clear enough soon enough. I just sat and was feeling how it was to find myself in this situation. I was excited and just happy. I missed my dogs though. I didn't want them to interfere with the peace and quiet around here during Oprah's stay. Three dogs are a handful and mine are little so they bark when they get excited about going for their morning walk, which would be now. In fact, I know that Oprah is a dog lover and I know she would love mine. What's more, I'm sure that she would love to bring hers up here the next time she comes. With that the door swung open and Oprah appeared.

"Good morning Sandra." Oprah was still not quite awake and was still rubbing her eyes as she continued to explain.

"I am usually a very early riser." Long pause as she made her way over to a chair and sat down. I just smiled at her and then offered, "Well, you know what they say about cottages. You sleep soundly at night and the fresh air makes you hungry during the day!"

"I hear you provide me with a justifiable excuse to overindulge while I'm here." And then she turned and looked around the property. Had a long stretch and then added, "And I plan to take advantage of it!" We laughed together.

"You and I together! First however, if you would like…" Then I switched my tone to that of an English accent, "I am offering you a personalized yoga class given by…" and I pointed to my chest and bowed my head, then finished the sentence, "Moi."

Oprah picked up quickly and then responded in her own version of an English accent and replied, "Oh that would be simply marvelous Sandra, simply marvelous!" We both laughed and then in her normal voice Oprah said, "I didn't bring anything to wear that would be suitable."

"I didn't think that you would so I took the liberty of placing some out on the dining room table."

"How did you know what size to get me Sandra?" I winked at her and smiled.

“I was guided.”

“Oh.” And she looked at me in that ‘not too sure where you got that information’ look. I then quickly spoke up with our itinerary for the day.

“First, get changed. Then we will have a quick stretch, some breakfast and then a visit with God in The Garden. Sound good?”

“Why indeed it does.” Oprah agreed. Looked around and then commented, “It's a perfect day for it isn't it?”

“Ordered up just for you! Now, when you can get your butt in gear, we'll do it up!”

“I'm a-movin!” With that she got up and went inside to change. In a few minutes she was already to go and the two of us walked around the cottage and headed down to the beach.

“Now, go easy on me” she cautioned.

“Not to worry” I assured her. Then explained, “I'll just watch you and then I'll get a pretty good idea at what level you are at and I will set the class accordingly.”

“Good.” she sounded pleased.

“Let us begin by sitting in Lotus position and we will begin the class with some big deep breaths.”

I began and Oprah was quick to follow. We spent a few minutes centering ourselves and for the next forty minutes or so, we had a great stretch. I was impressed by her ability. (O.K., now that comment WAS a suck-up!) I really have no idea how good at yoga Oprah is.

At the end of our class we both sat once again in our Lotus

position and went into a quiet meditation. We sat in silence for over ten minutes. Someone came by walking along the beach and we broke our concentration. Maybe they recognized her, or maybe they didn't. I would doubt it because who would look for her up at my cottage? No one, that's who. Oprah turned to me and said.

"Thank-you Sandra, that was lovely. I feel so calm and so refreshed."

"You did quite well at the meditation Oprah! Usually people are unable to sit in the quiet that long."

"Really, why is that?"

"I think it has to do with our thoughts taking us out of the moment."

She just nodded her head. Then she confessed to me, "Well to tell you the truth Sandra, my thoughts were not exactly on the sound of the waves."

"No?" I acted surprised.

"No. I was too much in the thoughts about what it was that you said yesterday about me becoming the first ordained royalty of America."

"Hmmm. I thought that you might have a few more questions concerning that." I paused and then said to her, "Oprah, I didn't plan to tell you that yesterday. In fact, I was going to curtsy to you on your show if I ever got to be on it. I kept seeing myself doing this and I had the knowing that there would be a coronation with you being made Queen. Truthfully, I think that God wants you to know this now and that your journey up here was not only to tell you more about you being Moses, but maybe like Moses, you are to be a recognized leader of your people. Oprah, your people are America."

She looked down at her hands and she picked up some sand and began to let it sift through her fingers. Then she said, "I hear what you are telling me and yet…" pause.

"And yet, what?" I urged her to speak on.

"And yet, I think that it just seems wild that your telling me this and then at the same time, deep inside of myself Sandra. I mean when I begin to put all the pieces in my life together and just as you said, perhaps, deep down, I have known that there was more. Yet, never did I put it all together until you said it to me. Sandra, do you think that is what is really going to take place? I just can't fathom it" Oprah concluded.

"Oprah" and I reached over and took her hands and turned myself to face her.

"Don't you worry about the *'how'*. You just focus on the part of you that knows what I told you about God's plan for you it true. Oprah, the people made you their Queen a long time ago. Think about it Oprah, they love you. America loves you, Oprah. They love you sooooo much that their love and their gratitude needs a form of expression into the physical form. You accepting this honor isn't a selfish thing or an egotistical thing. Oprah, this is a necessary thing."

"Necessary how" she wondered.

"Necessary because it will bring out the love of America. When Americans are given a reason to unit together there is no greater power on earth Oprah. America holds the most power in the world and that power is her people!"

I was quiet and then said, "Sadly, what we have come to believe that to express that muscle, that power, Americans need to do this in the form of war. Oprah, it's actually the opposite. If America is to be saved, if America is to regain its power, then Oprah, they must unite beside each other in love, not war." We smiled up at each other.

"Don't you see Oprah, you're America's hope. You hold all the power to give her back her true self. Oprah by accepting this job that God Himself is asking of you, you will unite your country in love and that love is the love that American has for their first Queen. To give this honor to one of their citizens will elevate the status of America. It will show the world that you have come of age. That America as a country can heal itself from its wounds and be more of a loving nation. A nation united in love for one another."

"Sandra, I can hear the wisdom of this and I know that yes, what you are telling me God wishes for America sounds amazing and I can picture it somewhat."

"Picture it! Man Oprah, when I was writing this book, you had a show on about Gay People Around the World. On it you had a man whose family was of royal decent. I can remember clearly how you told him that you were going to visit his country and have a word with his mother. Oprah, and by now I was speaking faster again with excitement and with knowing, "Oprah, it was evident. It was the validation that I was needing when I wrote this. Your little comment about how you're all about the palaces. Guess what? America will build you your own!"

I sat back and I placed my hand on top of my head and said, "And I can only imagine what a palace it will be! Oprah, America is known for its grandeur in entertainment, its sports. Nobody puts on a show like America! I can bet you that when America flexes its royal muscle, then, you better fasten your seat belt, cause Honey, you're gonna build yourself a palace!"

"Sandra, I just got goose bumps" Oprah piped in.

“So did I girlfriend, so did I!”

There was a pause and then she started to get excited as well.

“Sandra, I could hire all kinds of Americans to do the job!”

“Now you’re talking. Architects, builders, craftsmen and women.”

“Bricklayers, painters, artists, sculptures. Why we could do a show about the building of America's Royalty and have people in on the construction of the palace!”

“Not the palace Oprah, their palace. It will be a place for all of them to come.”

“Right, do you think it will be in Chicago?”

“I think America must decide where it would like its first royal family to live.”

“First royal family” she said slowly as it began to sink in.

“Oprah, it's like in England. Look how the people are governed now by the government, yet they are united under the Queen. Oprah, it is the Queen that unites the people, not the government. In most systems of government there is an opposition. That is the way it is. With this, everybody wins! Oprah you can be the one that represents the good about America and take that message to other countries. Even countries that are not open to our politics can be open to receiving her Queen. Oprah, you could reach the ears of so many heads of state that otherwise would be inaccessible. Just look at your broadcast that reached people all over the world. Oprah, you are loved by people world-wide.”

With that comment, I stood up, rubbed the sand off of my butt and my hands and said, “I'm hungry for breakfast. Let's go and eat!"

"Fine, I'm famished. All that yoga and talk of royalty has left me starving!"

"I told you the fresh air up here will make you hungry."

"What's for breakfast?"

"My homemade biscuits scrambled eggs and sausages."

"It sounds so good Sandra, I can't wait! But promise me one thing."

"What's that?"

"You won't tell Bob a thing about it!"

"You culinary preferences are safe with me Oprah." And with that, we stood up and made our way up to the cottage, chuckling along the way.

Chapter Twenty-Three

When we reached the cottage I went inside to prepare the food while her highness sat and enjoyed the lovely view from the terrace. It was a short time when I returned with our hot breakfast.

I opened the cottage door and said, "I always enjoy eating breakfast on the patio when I am at the cottage" I announced as I carried the food out the door and approached the table. As I looked up I saw that Oprah was resting on my lounger with her feet up and my book on Animal Speak resting opened on her lap.

Oprah spoke without looking up from the book, "It says here that the hawk through its flight communicates with humans and with the great creator spirit. It awakens our vision. It also says that 'hawk' will lead you to use your creative energy in manifesting your soul purpose."

"Also in this other book you have here Sandra, 'Medicine Cards' by Jamie Sams and David Carson that 'hawk' does represent messenger. That 'hawk' medicine teaches you to be observant, to look at your surroundings. Observe the obvious in everything that you do. Life is sending you signals. Sandra, I think that life has been sending me signals and perhaps I haven't been understanding them all! Well, at least now, with your in-put I am beginning to understand more."

Just then, someone jumped out from behind the corner of the cottage.

"Boo!"

"Chloe" I announced.

"Oprah, I would like to introduce to you my good friend, Chloe

MacDonald. Chloe is my cottage buddy and she and I have been such good friends…" I paused to count and then Chloe piped in, "Since I was like, eleven."

"Right and you're seventeen now so that would be about right. I have rented this place now for seven years."

"Chloe, Oprah."

Chloe just laughed and placed her hands behind her back and with a big smile said, Sondra, you don't have to tell me who she is, I already know!"

"Oh, well being the intelligent and oh so observant person that you are, I knew that you knew. Oprah is my friend and I asked her up here to spend some time with me and to see our lovely beach."

Oprah turned to me and asked with eyebrows raised, "Sondra?"

"It's Chloe's cottage name for me. She used to call me that as a little girl and I liked it, so it stuck."

"Humph."

Oprah directed her attention to Chloe and said, "It's lovely to meet you, Chloe. Do you come up here every summer as well?"

"Heck no Oprah, I live up here."

"All year" Oprah asked.

"Yup. It's the most beautiful place in the whole world."

"I agree with you whole-heartedly, Chloe."

"Chloe, I am so glad that you came over for a visit. However, we are just about to eat our breakfast and Oprah and I have a very busy day planned."

"I know. I just wanted to come over and meet her" Chloe blushed. Then Oprah said to her, "Well, I'm ever so glad that you did Chloe."

"Well, bye Sondra. Bye Oprah."

Oprah and I both simultaneously said. "Good-bye Chloe!"

As she walked across the lawn Oprah bent over to me and said in her English accent, "Oh Sondra, she is beautiful!" I chuckled and then answered, "Isn't she?" I knew when she was at a very young age that she would be a knock-out."

"She looks like a cross between Tara Banks and Mariah Carrey, don't you think?"

"I told her that one day she was going to be a model."

"Oh yes indeed. Is she modeling now?"

"We tried to hook her up once with some company, last year in fact. Nothing so far. Honestly Oprah, if she was able to get to the right people" and with my eye brows raised, shaking my head in the affirmative I added in a very leading way, "If only I knew the right people" then looked at her.

"I could make some calls." Oprah willingly offered.

"Good. Oh Oprah, she is such a sweetie and I know that she would be such a natural at it. I have only one concern."

"Which is?"

"Well, she is young and fairly naive. I would hate for her to get hooked up with the wrong people."

"Not to worry Sandra. Just leave everything to me."

"I knew you would be able to help Oprah."

"Ah, let's eat now, before this food gets cold" She said as she pulled her chair up to the table.

We ate our breakfast and had casual conversation. Oprah interrupted on several occasions and remarked about how delicious the food was. After we had finished, she said as she pushed her plate away.

"My compliments to the chef."

I nodded my head in recognition of said compliment and asked if she would like her tea now?

"Yes please."

Chapter Twenty-Four

With that I cleared the table and returned with two teas. We both turned our chairs to face the Garden and I began to explain exactly what it was that I had learned about the Garden of Eden.

"Now Oprah, there are a number of things that I need to fill you in on first" I preloaded our conversation.

"I am here to learn, Sandra - fire away."

With that I began my story.

"Oprah, when I come up to this place, I rest. I sit. I read and do some yoga. Write my journals and be with God. The way to be with God is to first of all, be alone. When you are quiet you can listen for His voice."

"Right. I remember you sharing that with me yesterday."

"Now, what I am about to share with you is how I communicate with God. I am not suggesting that my way is the only way that you or anyone else for that matter will find your way to God in His Garden. After all, we have our own paths and our own journeys. Agreed?"

"Agreed."

"This is my pathway and my logic explained."

"O.K., shoot."

"If you believe that the Bible is God's living word, and it is just as relevant today as it was when it was written, then you must conclude that God is still alive and watching over us."

"O.K." she said.

"So, if God is just as alive now as He was then, and seeing that He is once again making Himself known to us once more, I believe the same rules have to apply."

"Which rules?"

"In order to gain entrance into the Garden of Eden today Oprah, take the sequence of events that lead to our expulsion and reverse them."

"Huh?"

"Take the instructions from the Bible and follow it backwards to the beginning. Cause what happened then is happening now. The (and here I made parenthesis in the air with my fingers) 'As it was in the beginning stuff'. You know 'Is now until the end. The first is that last and the last shall be the first kind of thing.'

"What do you mean?"

"Well Oprah, look at the sequence of events. We are in the Garden, eat the Forbidden Fruit, out of the Garden."

"Ah huh."

"Reverse it. We are out of the Garden. Eat the Forbidden fruit, we are back in the Garden!"

Oprah was not saying anything. So, I went on.

"At this time in our world, we are finding ourselves out of the Garden. Someone such as myself who has been with God, in the garden, comes forward only to report that entrance is once again achievable."

“Alerting others of the phenomenon” she quickly responded, as Oprah was listening intently.

“Right. Now people are coming forward with more and more stories or reported miracles.”

“Indicating God’s presence is close?”

“Very. When we ate the fruit…” I paused and then caught myself, “I mean, when I ate the fruit” and I then pointed to my chest only to notice Oprah nodding up and down in agreement as she then said, “Yes, that’s right. Let us all not forget who got us into this mess.”

“Fine! When I ate the fruit, Oprah, there was something in that fruit that contained access to a higher knowledge. You must eat of the Forbidden Fruit in order to once again receive that higher knowledge and regain entrance.”

“So, have you found it? The Forbidden Fruit that contains the knowledge?”

“Yes, I have. When consumed, it gives you temporary access. At least for me it does. Then after awhile, you begin to leave the Garden again as the affect of the fruit wears off.”

“So, what fruit is it that we are talking about here Sandra?”

“Well, think about it. What knowledgeable fruit is forbidden?”

“I don’t know. I have to think about it for a moment.”

I gave her a few seconds.

“I will put it this way to you, Oprah. Ask God Himself to guide you to it. It may be different for others and I would not like my discovery to be an absolute. I mean my intention is not to taint people's view or at worst, lead them on a path other than the one God has laid out for them."

"What a cop-out Sandra. Do you mean to tell me that you're not gonna tell me now that I have come all the way up here what the Forbidden Fruit is?"

"That's right. Sorry Oprah, but I will give you a clue."

"O.K. I'll bite. What's the clue?"

"It can be eaten or not eaten."

Oprah repeated out loud after me at a slower pace, "It can be eaten or not eaten."

"That's right and that is all I am going to tell you."

Oprah looked at me in a manner that would suggest that she was miffed at me. I rallied back with, "Come on, I'll walk you through the steps that lead into the Garden, and you can make up your mind if you're going in or not."

Chapter Twenty-Five

I got up from my chair and so did Oprah. I took in a big breath and said, "O.K., first of all, there are some things that you need to take in with you.

"Such as what, Sandra?"

"Such as a pillow for your head and a blanket or towel so as to keep warm or cover yourself up with when the sun hits the Garden. It depends on what time of day it is and how long you are planning to spend. If you eat the fruit, you'll be there a good two hours or more. Next, I always take in a journal."

"Why is that?"

"That is because when I am talking with God, he usually likes me to write down what it is that He would like me to know. Sometimes, He gives me so much information! You'll want to remember as much as you can about what is said, so write it down!"

Oprah repeated slowly what it was that she needed.

"So, I take in a pen and my journal and I write down what I am hearing."

"Right. Oprah, you may not write a thing once you are with God and in His presence. It will all depend on what is meant to happen for you."

"O.K. I gotcha. No expectations."

"Your ability to hear what God is telling you is in direct correlation with how 'present' you can remain. The key to this entire process is not to doubt the first voice that you hear."

"Why is that?"

"Because the first voice - if you listen for it - is the voice of God speaking. Don't argue with it or try to rationalize or get into intellectualizing. Just listen and believe."

"So allow the first voice you hear to be O.K. and not to argue or question what it is saying. Just be in a state of believing?"

"Yes. Oprah. Yes. And remember the voice will come from within."

"You mean within me?"

"Yes. You will feel it. Not just think it. Oprah, when in God's presence, do not doubt what it is that you are receiving. Give yourself permission that when you're alone with God in the Garden, not to doubt. For just that two or three, or four hour period, promise yourself not to judge what knowing that He is placing inside of you." With that I reached out and placed my hands on either side of her arms and directed her "And then just allow it to happen."

"Allow what to happen?"

"Allow all the messages to be true."

"But what if I do not believe in what it is that God is telling me? What if it doesn't make any sense? What if it's crazy? What if it's the Forbidden Fruit talking?"

"Now those are questions from someone who is in the fear. If you approach this with fear in your heart, I can pretty much guarantee that nothing is what you will experience, Oprah."

"Why is that?"

“Cause fear is a lower vibration and you want to be vibrating higher to match the Garden’s frequency. The Fruit helps with that.”

I turned to her and said, “If all things happen for a reason, then trust in it! Trust that this too is meant to be. Oprah, you would not have come here if you were not meant to hear what it is that I am telling you. If your feelings are screaming at you that what I’m proposing is wrong for you, then listen to those feelings.”

“So, if I am not comfortable with it, I don't have to try it?”

“Of course not! Don't forget that this is my work and my journey. It is meant to be shared with others so that they too may find a way to be one with God. Oprah, the Forbidden Fruit really does help to release the world of the physical for me, and helps me enter the world of the spirit quickly. I will confess to you that over the years, I have not been able to park my responsibilities and go and sit with learned masters and devote my existence entirely to my spiritual journey. I exist in the world of the physical. I am a mom with kids for heaven sake! And until God is ready to move me into a permanent state of bliss again, well, all I can tell you is that I am in reality, Oprah!”

We both laughed at that.

“O.K. Sandra, I can hear you. I still don't know if I'm gonna try it your way or not.”

“That's fine Oprah. You must trust how it is that you are feeling. That is the only way that you can decide what is right for you. Agreed?”

“Agreed. So, go on.”

“Fine. So, to recap, I gather up my journal, pen, pillow and towel.

Usually I grab a water bottle. Sometimes I take my Ipod and listen to music as well. It just depends on what it is that I feel."

"Got it."

"Now, this is the time I usually eat the fruit. Take my stuff and go down to the Garden where my hammock awaits."

I am walking towards the Garden now with Oprah and I am continuing with my instructions.

"So, let's continue" Oprah began to recap.

"I've got my blanket, my water, my journal and I am eating the fruit or not." Oprah smiled at me and I at her.

"Hey, you know what? I just thought of something. Why do you think it was Eve that had to first eat the Forbidden Fruit? Why wasn't it Adam?"

"I don't know Sandra. I never really gave it much thought."

"Do you think that it may have been the sequence of things?"

"You mean, like a code to the unraveling of the mysteries of the exiting and entering into the Garden of Eden?"

"Well, yeahahhh." We laughed at that one.

"I mean it could have been Eve." I turned to her and bowed my head as I said, "I mean, Moi that first ate of the fruit because it was again, a clue for us now that the women were to be the ones to lead us all into the obtaining of the knowledge of The Garden?"

"What are you getting at Sandra?"

"I don't know for sure, but I am surmising that perhaps it was because it is women who are the ones that are to get us back in the Garden because they are the ones that got us out."

"Interesting. Humph. I'll have to think about that one" Oprah offered.

"Well, why do you think that God would choose a woman to be America's first Queen instead of it being a King?"

"I guess it's because..." Oprah stopped and thought for a moment to formulate her answer.

"Maybe it's because we are needing to balance the energies of male and female."

"Yeah. Makes sense."

"Maybe it is up to the Eve's, the Dorothy's, the Oprah's of this world to begin this journey towards the knowledge that will change the way we do things now, not unlike the situation in the original Garden of Eden."

"Right. So, maybe that is because women are to be the first to awaken and then as Eve did, pass the knowledge onto their partners."

"Could be Sandra, interesting thought."

"Yeah."

We both paused, lost in our thoughts and then I snapped to attention and said, "O.K., now where was I? Oh yeah, we are now heading towards the Garden. Now, Oprah I want to point out at the onset that this is My Garden. Not necessarily 'Thee' Garden."

Oprah began to shake her head and pointed her finger at me as she uttered, “You can protest all that you want Sandra, but I still think that it is thee “Garden of Eden”.

“Fine, think what you will, I just know that God has spoken with me and has assured me that He will come to visit each and every Garden that is built with the intention of creating a place to be still and commune with Him.”

“Why it sounds as if God’s Holy Spirit is just like Santa Claus” She said in a smart tone.

“As a matter of fact smarty, I think that is a great example and quite frankly, the whole idea!”

“We hang up our own stockings and Father Christmas arrives, we build our own Garden of Eden and God’s spirit comes.”

“Really Sandra, it is the best example to give to people isn’t it?”

“God's Garden is anywhere that you can commune with God for two to four hours without being disturbed. It can be at your home in your own backyard. It can be in a park, by the water. Or it can be at a campsite, a cottage. Anywhere that you can kick back and be at peace. I happen to have this place as my Garden because it is up here that I can leave behind all of my troubles and worries for while. I can come up here and just relax.”

We both stopped and took in a deep breath as I told her just breath in and allow the peace to enter into you.”

We stood and breathed together. All of a sudden, standing right there on the lawn, I received a rather sudden image in my mind and said, “Oprah, have you ever heard of a spiritual birthday?”

“A spiritual birthday” Oprah repeated and then asked, “What Sandra, is a spiritual birthday?”

As we both stood out on the lawn in the sun, I decide to explain it to her seeing that the image of it just popped into my head.

Chapter Twenty-Six

"About five years ago, I was up here on my own. It was about the time that I began to receive messages, signs from God that I was His messenger. It was July 25th. I started the day by sitting outside up there on the patio. It was around nine o'clock I believe and I spotted a wren."

I paused and looked down.

"In fact, I believe I spotted it right here exactly. Now, to begin with Oprah" and I looked right at her as I went on with my story, "This was quite unusual because wrens rarely appear in the open. You usually can only catch a glimpse of them at either dawn or dusk. It was about 9 am."

"So, did you go and look up wren in your Animal Speak book?"

"Sharp as a tack you are Oprah! That is exactly what I did. I opened my Animal Speak and looked up wren and it is the bird that represents The Virgin Mary."

Oprah raised her eye brow at this as I went onto tell her, "Right away I knew that her presence was being made known to me through the visit from the bird."

"Really?"

"Anyways, I ate my breakfast that morning and just as I was finishing, some kids, Chloe and her brothers as well as two cousins, all came racing around the corner to visit me. Curtis, the littlest one, came to show me that he had found an empty robin's egg and held it out to show me. I immediately got the message that he was showing me an empty tomb."

"Why did you think 'empty tomb' Sandra?"

“I didn't think it, the knowing of it just popped into me. I choose not to argue with the message. I just let the energy and the moment continue to flow in hopes that more information would be given to me. So, the kids had all come over to see my picture that the cousin’s mom had painted for me the day before. Her name is Nadine Harper. She is an artist and my good friend Laura's sister. Laura is Chloe's mom.”

Oh, O.K., I got it.”

“So, I went inside and got the painting. I was standing in the door way of the cottage and I held up the picture. All the kids, and Laura who had joined us at that time, all smiled and pointed at the picture and said, “Look at the star!”. I had never noticed the star before and had to look at it again. Sure enough Oprah, I could see in the picture a large yellow star - as plain as day.”

“You didn't notice it before this?”

“Nope. Didn’t see that at all.”

Oprah listened intently.

“After they had all admired the picture they went off back to Laura’s. I didn't think any more of it and went about doing my morning routine which consisted of some yoga stretches and some light reading. I made myself some lunch and had some lemonade. As I sat down I noticed that a ladybug had landed on my drinking glass. I reached for my Animal Speak book and immediately looked up ladybug.”

“What did it tell you?”

“Ladybug is a beetle and it means resurrection.”

I continued on after I had asked Oprah if she was sure she didn’t want to sit back down on the patio or not. She declined.

“So, I began to put together the events of the day, the puzzle pieces I like to call them and began to see what the universe was trying to tell me.”

I counted on my fingers “One, The Virgin Mary's visit through the wren. Two, an empty tomb. Three, the appearance of a star and Four, the message of resurrection. I thought to myself that this day was beginning to look a lot like Christmas.”

“I’d say Easter too” Oprah blurted out.

Oprah was very correct.

“Easter too!” I agreed.

“So, I began to feel and to sense that this was a birth day of some kind. Now Oprah, get this, I walked over to Laura's for a visit later on that day and guess who is sitting on the front lawn painting another picture? Nadine.”

“Hey Nadine, how are you doing?”

“Good, how about you?”

“Amazing” I told her.

“Yeah, you seem so happy Sandra, is today your birthday or something?”

“Well, Oprah” when I heard her ask that I knew immediately it was another sign. “How so?”

“Because it was somewhat of a leap to assume it could be someone’s birthday just because a person was in a good mood. So, inside of myself I smiled at it because I no longer was going to doubt the powerful energy that was guiding me that day. The universe was showing me something and I was in the flow of it.”

“It kind of sounds as if you were on a spiritual treasure hunt or something Sandra.”

“Yes, it does. And it felt like it too Oprah. So much was coming to me that I just sat back and let it all happen. Like I was being led from one clue to another. So, get this. I then asked her what she was painting and she said she wasn't sure cause she hadn't finished it yet but it was a painting that she was to call "The Birth Day". Not because it was someone's birthday, but because it was a day of a birth! Oprah, I was wigging out inside cause I knew again that this too was a sign.”

“Now that is really cool, Sandra. You were feeling like it was a day of birth for you and this woman just happened to be in the process of painting a picture entitled, 'The Birth Day.'”

“I know Oprah, I know.” Now I was really getting into telling her the story and she was just as into hearing it! What fun!”

“Oprah, I ended up visiting with everyone for awhile. I had received enough signs to know that it was indeed a birthday - my spiritual birthday - is what the energy told me. I even had the nerve to tell everyone that it was my spiritual birthday that day.”

“What did they say when you told them that Sandra?”

“Actually, they just smiled at me and said, “That’s great!”

“Did they question you or ask what the heck is a spiritual birthday?”

“No. I think that is because up at the cottage we were used to playing games of all sorts and this was my game. In all honesty Oprah, they simply just accepted what I was telling them without question. It was as if on a higher spiritual level, they knew enough to play along and were in the flow of the supernatural just as I was."

"Well, yes. It would appear so wouldn't it? I mean they were after all, with you in this. I mean it wasn't just happening to you alone. They too had a part in it."

"Yes. I think that is what made it all so real. Cause it was really happening and not just to me. Anyways, Laura and her sister were having dinner together that evening and had asked if I would come. I agreed and then offered to go into town and buy the kids a small gift and to also get a spiritual birthday cake for dessert."

"Really?"

"Yup."

"You actually were gonna go and buy yourself a spiritual birthday cake?"

"Why not? Look Oprah, I was in the energy of that like a child entering heaven. I didn't doubt or question the goings on of the day, I just went with the flow of it."

"Amazing. I mean it Sandra. That just blows me away that you were that open to just be with what was going on, no matter how absurd and impossible it maybe!"

"I know." I smiled at the compliment.

"And of course all the kids were loving it too cause up at the cottage any excuse to have a birthday party is a good excuse."

We both smiled. Then Oprah asked me, "So, did anything else unusual happen?"

"Yes. I loaded up all the kids into my car and went into town. We first stopped at my friend's jewelry store. I took the kids in and was chatting with my friend about how it was my spiritual birthday and without even thinking twice she handed me over this pair of earrings that were made in the likeness of a pair of feet! And if that wasn't enough, she then gave to me another single earring which was a small pink ladybug!"

"No, Sandra, really, a ladybug?" Oprah was amazed. Then she added, "Didn't you just say that a lady bug visited you at lunch time? Then you end up getting a lady bug earring. That is so strange!"

"Yes, and what's more, she just gave them to me as a gift!" I turned to face her, then continued.

"I first thought, Humph? Feet, I'm a Reflexologist, maybe that's the message contained in the gift? Then no! Oprah, the knowing came into me instantly I receive the feet because I am following in the footsteps of Christ! Oprah, it was like I was in this dream world again where everybody was acting normal, but not."

"How normal is it for a shopkeeper to just hand over free merchandise? And for a spiritual birthday nonetheless!"

"Exactly Oprah. That's what I thought."

"Next we went to the dollar store and afterwards, to the grocery store. I had the baker write 'Happy First Spiritual Birthday Sandra' on one of their cakes."

"You know what I found to be strange, Oprah?"

"I am waiting to hear what YOU consider strange, Sandra!"

"Very funny. What I found strange is that no one even asked me what a spiritual birthday even was."

"Well what is a spiritual birthday?"

"It is given to you by God first of all. Second, you never know what day it will be when it comes. It will come when you are in the knowing of who it is that you were, who it is that you are and what it is that God would have you do this lifetime."

"O.K." Oprah nodded, still digesting this.

"Oprah, when I got to Laura's sisters for dinner, it was a humble cottage. When I say humble cottage Oprah, I'm talking h.u.m.b.l.e., humble."

"That bad, eh?"

"We're talking bugs on the floor humble."

"Yeah but Sandra, were they ladybugs?" Oprah snickered at this.

"You're getting to be quiet the wisenheimer aren't you Winfrey?

"I'm just following the story" was her weak attempt to cover up her lame joke.

I cleared my throat and continued on, "I knew this was my spiritual birthday and I knew that the day had now taken on a striking resemblance to Jesus' birth story."

"So what happened at dinner?"

"The kids had all got me a spiritual birthday present. I did not expect that whatsoever!"

"What did you get?"

"An empty heart box. And a Christmas candle."

“A Christmas candle, in the middle of summer?”

“Exactly what I thought too Oprah! It was such a sign. People giving me gifts. I mean the earrings from the jewelers. A pair of feet, following in the footsteps of Jesus. Ladybugs, meaning resurrection. Oprah, what a day rich in the spirit.”

“I'll say, how did you know what it all meant, Sandra?"”

Such a good question, Oprah.” I paused and pondered.

“I believe that it was a message not just for me though Oprah, but for us all. I am believing that when a person is to be born again, then they are spiritually born. They come into the awareness of who it is that they are and what it is that they are here to do. Once they have received that knowing, look for God to bring you your spiritual birthday.”

“So are you suggesting that everyone will have stars and wrens and gold Christmas candles?”

“I am saying that the components of Christ's birthday and Easter will be present, they just may appear in a different form.”

“So if I were to have a spiritual birthday, it could be very different from yours?”

“Very different indeed. It will be interesting to see if others once awakened will also find that they too have been give spiritual birthdays.”

“Hold on, I have to go to the washroom before we go into the Garden.” With that, Oprah quickly walked up to the cottage once again. I called out to her as she left, “You're not going to have any fruit are you?”

Her back was to me and I watched as she raised her arm in

acknowledgement that I has spoken to her. She didn’t stop or turn around which indicated to me that she had to go now!

Chapter Twenty-Seven

In five minutes, she was back.

“O.K., O.K. Sandra, let's get going with this Garden thing!” Oprah was waving her arms and getting herself psyched up for this.

“All right then, let's do it!” I took Oprah to the opening of the Garden.

“Now, look around you and marvel at the beauty of this place and breathe in all the colors and the energy.”

We both took in some deep breaths. I continued on with my instructions as to how to enter the Garden. Then I reached out and held her hand and said to her in a whisper, “Hey Oprah, you're gonna meet God and actually speak with Him. Aren't you just freaking out? I mean this is it. This is the time that you have been thinking about since you read my book and now it is actually happening.”

“I know, I know. I am really excited Sandra and a little nervous to boot. What am I going to say to Him? What if I don't get anything?”

“Hey! Stop that. Just let go of all expectations and let whatever happens, happen.” Then I whispered with assurance, “You'll do great. Remember, no doubts, no judgments. O.K.?”

“Fine.” She took in a deep breath and squeezed my hands. Then she said, “I'm ready, let's go.” And with that the two of us made our way down the rabbit hole.

“I usually will start to sing some kind of song about how beautiful this place is or how grateful I am to be entering into

God's presence."

"Sing?"

"Yup. It doesn't matter if it's a song or not. I just start to sing about how wonderful God is and how amazing His creation is. I make it up as I go along. And every time it's different."

"Why is it always different?

"That's because, every time I come here to be with God, it is a different time and I am coming from a different place. There is no room for rote behavior in The Garden Oprah. Being in the moment means being with how it is that you are at this moment. So, Oprah, how are you at this moment?"

Oprah was thinking about this and after a short time she replied, "Nervous. Grateful for this time with you, Sandra and so wonderfully excited to meet with God Himself and have His full light and attention upon me."

"That's a good start. Now say those exact words only this time, sing them. Use whatever melody that comes to you. Sometimes, I don't even follow a melody, I just sing."

Oprah and I began to sing. She was singing and I was listening for a moment. I could sense how shy she had become. She looked over at me with a look that said "Am I doing this right?" I then quickly began to accompany her. It was amazingly good, considering. We sang for about a minute or two.

"Good. O.K. now, I want you to come over here and imagine that we are standing at some gates."

"What kind of gates?"

"Heaven's Gates."

"Oprah, imagine that right here in front of us is Saint Peter himself. Now, close your eyes, and try to picture what he would look like. I envision my friend John Ross. I believe that he has the energy of Saint Peter in him."

"One of your friends is Saint Peter?"

I could tell by the expression upon her face that she was just hit with one more thing and in surrender she confided, "I'm just not going to say anything." She held up both hands in that stop gesture and shook her head as she continued on.

"I'm just gonna accept all that you say from here on in."

"It's the best way to be Oprah.

"Sandra, if you are crazy, then I'm in your world. I am through the Looking Glass now and I don't really care much more about anything else. Lead on MacDuff!" and she raised her arm to signal a charge. I then further instructed her, O.K. So, now, get down on your knees, close your eyes and ask that Saint Peter reveal himself to you."

Oprah complied, somewhat hesitantly.

"You mean I have to get down on my knees for this?"

"Or just one knee, whatever feels right at the time." She looked at me as if this was asking a little bit much. However, she held onto my arm and the two of us got down on our knees. I looked over at her and said, "Well, you want to see how it's done for real don't you?" She just looked at me. I smartly advised her, "Sometimes even kings and queens have to show some humility!"

I got a real look at that one, then continued on.

"Now, close your eyes and ask Saint Peter to make Him known to you." Oprah obliged me and closed her eyes. I was watching her face now and I waited for about thirty seconds until I saw her smile.

"Who do you see as Saint Peter?"

She opened her eyes and turning to me began to laugh.

"All I can think about is Sydney Poitier!"

I smiled broadly back at her and then said "Good. That's great. If that is what you see, don't argue with it. Just let it be O.K." I was sensing that Oprah was not taking this very seriously and decided to impress upon her the importance of this entering of the Garden.

"Oprah, this isn't a joke you know. You really are entering onto holy ground."

"Holy ground?" She nodded in understanding. Then she took in a deep breath as if she was mustering up all the sanctity she could.

"Well, yeah, it is where God dwells. It is where you will, and as best as you can, be perfect before the Lord. You see, Oprah, when God sees us, He sees the light of Himself inside of us. If our light is weak, then we are covered in our transgressions for we have not sought forgiveness for our sins."

"So, asking for the forgiveness of our sins in mandatory?"

"Yes because we are cleaning ourselves up so that God can find our light. We still must confess before we enter. It matters that we are acknowledging our imperfection and are bowing to His authority. We are His servants and when a servant comes before his/ her master, she bows."

I then felt another recap was in order.

“Now, in order to gain entrance into God's garden, we are following the sequence. Eat fruit. Come to the entrance of your Garden. Sing praises to God. Next, imagine that you are standing in front of the gates to heaven. Close your eyes and ask that Saint Peter who is standing at the entrance make himself known to you.”

“Got it!”

“Right. Bow your head, ask for forgiveness of your sins and ask to be washed clean from your transgressions. I usually say something like: 'Saint Peter, remove from me my iniquities and my wrong doings. Make me presentable to God. Clean me from head to toe. Make me like a shinny penny without tarnish. May I be presentable to Him so that he will be able to see my heart.'”

Oprah turned to me and smiled and said, “That's lovely, Sandra.”

I smiled back and said, “Whatever your heart is saying, say it to Saint Peter.”

“Do I say this out loud?”

“I do. I don't scream it or sing this part. I just quietly pray, knowing that Saint Peter is listening to me.”

“O.K.”

“Now, ask Saint Peter for entrance into the Garden. Now bow your head and wait.”

“Wait for what?”

“If you bow your head and wait, you will feel a hand upon your head and then you know that you’re good to go.”

"" will feel a hand upon my head?"

"Yup. I paused and looked up at her and then said, "Just do it!"

We both lowered our heads and waited in silence. Suddenly, Oprah reached over and grabbed my arm in a vice grip as she whispered, "Sandra, I feel it, I feel it!"

I could tell by her voice that she was elated. I whispered under my breath at her, "Told you."

We raised our heads and then I said, "Good, now we can go in."

We both stood up, holding onto one another for support. As we made our way into the heart of the Garden we held fast onto one another's hand. I lead her up to my hammock which was strung up between two trees.

"Now, you just slide up into the hammock and I will hold your things."

I helped hold her towel and her journal, pen etc. while she wrestled with getting into the hammock. Finally, she was in and I handed to her all the paraphernalia in my hands.

"Comfy?"

"Yes, very."

Oprah was smiling and took in a deep breath and closed her eyes. I could tell she was bringing herself into the moment. Then she asked me, "Should I still sing something?"

"If you like. Are you feeling moved to do this? I do know from experience Oprah, that God really does love to be sung to! He responds best when we sing our praises or our requests to Him rather than just speak them. He told me that one day, so I do my best to come before the Lord with praise and thanksgiving."

"You're just saying thanks for everything."

"Yeah. And also telling Him how great He is. He likes that stuff. So, just do it. Give to Him what He asks of you."

"Sounds simple enough."

"Sometimes in The Garden, I will just sing my thoughts and praises to God for however long I feel that I would like to do this. Other times, He may begin right away with a conversation, or message that He wishes for me to know about. Oprah, now is YOUR private time with God. You could sing or just start to speak to Him. Whatever happens, trust that what is happening is meant to be. Don't judge it good or bad."

"Got it."

"Be alert and you will sense His presence when He arrives. Now if you look up there, through those trees, right at the top of that one" as I pointed upwards.

"That is where God comes in. At least for me."

"So He enters in from there?"

"Yes, you may find it different for you. You'll just have to wait and see. Now, you can start. Oh, yeah, and sometimes, when I am feeling particularly affectionate, I will call Him, Yahweh."

"Yahweh" Oprah questioned.

"That's the personal name that you use to speak with Him. His title is God, His name is Yahweh."

“I didn’t know that Sandra.”

“I just use it when I feel it. Most of the time I use God, or Father.”

“Got it!”

“O.K., I'm just going to leave you in here for awhile now Oprah, on your own.”

“On my own?” she sounded concerned.

“There is no need for anything to happen or not happen, Oprah. Just be with this place and be in the energy. Relax. Now just begin to breath and to be in this moment and remember...” I couldn't get the rest of my sentence out and Oprah was finishing it with “Don't judge or label. Just watch and be in nature.”

“Not only are you a Queen, you are also a very good student.”

“About all that queen stuff. I was going to ask God's word on that while I was in here.”

“Good plan. Now wait and see if it is God's plan. Ask Him for validation.”

“What kind of validation?”

“Just ask Him for a sign.”

I smiled at her and then reassured her, “If you need me, I'll be on a walk or over at the neighbor's or something. You'll have complete privacy for at least two hours, O.K.?”

“Yup.”

“I’ll see you in a few hours.”

With that I turned my back and headed out of the Garden leaving Oprah laying in the hammock, staring up at the sky. I said a little prayer to myself.

“Heavenly Lord, whatever it is that you would have Oprah know this day, I pray that you will guide her and keep her safe during this special time. Help her to trust in you and all that she receives.”

With that, I walked up to the cottage, put on my hat and glasses. Loaded on some sun screen and went for a walk.

Chapter Twenty-Eight

I had some time to reflect upon my two days with Oprah and marveled how even I didn't know what God had in store for her. I thought about how exciting it was that she was going to be finally given the proper title she has earned. I brought along with me my Ipod and began to listen to some of my favorite tunes as I enjoyed a few hours of peace and not talking.

What was really great for me was the time that I now had to myself. You see, I know that God is with us at all times. I know that He is with me on my walk and at the same time is also with Oprah. That's what is so cool about God, he can be everywhere and know everything about us. Just like Santa Claus.

I laughed out loud at that one.

So many times when I am writing for God, I can see Him in a Santa Suit! I think that is because He wants to convey that loving Father image to me. It appeals to my inner child and when I see Him in that manner, I know He is telling me to trust in Him as a child would trust in Santa. It really is a lovely message.

I raised my face towards the sun and breathed in the smell of the lake. I felt so good, so at peace with myself and all that had transpired between us.

After I walked all the way to the point where the cottages end, I then turned around and headed back. It took me a little over two hours and when I returned headed up to the cottage where I helped myself to a cold drink. I was wondering whether my guest was still in heaven or not and I sneaked a peek out the back door. There, back on my lounge chair, her head buried in my Animal Speak book was her majesty herself!

"Hey there! How are you feeling? Heavenly?"

I was met with “I am unbelievable!” she announce in a voice that was peaceful and serene.

“Good chat with God?”

“Great chat with God.” With that she put down the book. Do you know that there was a blue jay, a cardinal, and a rabbit?”

Really, so lot's of visitors?”

“I'll say. And I kept seeing shapes of elephants in the clouds as I was staring up into the sky.”

“Elephants? They are associated with royalty, Oprah! I believe you just had a validation on that queen thing!”

Excitedly, she continued on with her story. “I am just looking up the meaning of these and it is unbelievable that they are bringing me the same message that God did, that you did as well, Sandra.”

“Really? How about that.” I kept the sarcasm to a minimum.

“So, you got to speak with Him eh?”

“Yup. That's not all. I received some pretty good stuff of my own.”

“Anything that you would like to share?”

“Just that there is more to this day than we both realize and that much good will come out of my visit up here and your book Sandra.”

“That's good. I'm really glad that you did well. Hungry?”

“Starved.”

"You keep on reading and I'll just make us a quick snack."

"Well Sandra, wait a minute, don't you want to know what God told me?"

"Well, yeah. I was hoping that you would share that information over lunch. I was just concerned that you would be as hungry as I am and that naturally, you would share you story over lunch."

"Well, hurry up and grab us something, I am busting to tell you all about it!"

I went inside and quickly began to make us both a tuna fish sandwich. While I was doing this, my son Doug called. He told me about a change in plans. After the phone call I yelled out the window at Oprah, "Change of plans. Gayle wants to come up with Doug and pick you up."

Oprah looked up confused, then said, "I thought I was to meet her back in Oakville at your home?"

"Well, yes that was the plan. Apparently after you called last night and told her about this place, she wants to come up and see for herself. So, what did you tell her?"

"Just that it was the most beautiful and peaceful place on the planet."

"Don't you think that's a bit of an exaggeration?" I laughed.

"Well, once you hear what it is that I learned from God Himself, I don't think that is an exaggeration Sandra. Not one little bit."

"O.K. then. Doug said that they were leaving for here now, so we have about three hours left on our own."

I turned to go back and finish the task at hand. Within a short time I was carrying out our lunch onto the patio only to find Oprah standing there, just looking back at the Garden. We sat down and devoured our meal in short order. Not much was said during that time. We were both just quiet and exchanged pleasantries regarding the fare. As we were nearing the end, I refilled her lemonade and then sat back in my chair and said, "Alright then, let's have it. What did He say?"

Oprah took in a deep breath and then exhaled and began her story.

"First of all, when you left me there, I sang to God, just as you told me. After a few minutes, I just stopped singing and was quiet. I became aware of all the beauty around me and I just breathed it in. Truly Sandra, I was being in the moment! Then like a picture show, I saw our flashes of our time here together. Then a wave of knowing, as you say Sandra, came over me and was aware of many truths."

"Like what?" I was hanging on her every word.

"About me being who it is that you say I am. Queen Oprah. It feels right. I'm overcoming my embarrassment with regards to your prediction and I can see the good that will come from it. I can see that I am already leading the country in a spiritual direction. I definitely feel the love that people have for me. I see it every day in their eyes. Sandra, I am already there, yet without the recognition or title."

"You will be amazed Oprah, how once that ceremony/coronation takes place how quickly your energy will adjust to the new appointment" I quickly added.

"Yes, I believe you are right. Oh, Sandra, it is all so obvious to me now! All I can think of is the good I could do as Queen. How it is that I could travel and meet with all the different leaders of the world in hopes of helping them to also awaken." I couldn't contain myself any longer and added, "Not to mention what positive energy, what positive LOVE energy that it would produce! It would raise us all to a higher vibration. People would all unite in their love for you. It is something most people are already feeling for you Oprah."

"That stuff about erecting a palace Sandra. I got a big "Yes" feeling for that as well."

"Awesome! I also have a feeling that there is more to building this palace than meets the eye."

"Why, what did you get?"

"I just have a feeling that the building of this palace means more. I'm feeling it has something to do with the Bible and God and the House of David."

"Can you be any more specific Sandra" Oprah asked.

"No. It'll come when it's ready. But I am definitely getting that there is a strong connection between the two events." I

took in a deep breath and then asked her anxiously.

"So, what is it that you received in the Garden from God?"

"Sandra, I know that you will not find this as unbelievable as I do! In fact, I wouldn't even begin to know what would be unbelievable to you."

"Ha-Ha. I stated straight faced in a monotone voice." She ignored me and kept on talking as she was smiling like a Cheshire cat.

"But I'm still buzzin."

"What, what are you going to tell me?" I looked at her and slowly added, "You're not going to tell me that you got a new ten commandments or anything like that are you?"

Oprah's eyebrows lifted and her eyes widened and her mouth hung open for a moment and I just blurted out, "That's it! Isn't it Oprah? That's it, isn't it? You got another ten commandments!"

"I'm past amazement and bordering on insanity here. You're killing me Sandra, your killing me! How did you guess that?"

"It's under the 'obvious' Oprah." I was nodding my head up and down and mirroring her smile. Then I said in an urgent voice, "Well, come on! Let's hear it!"

"Man." Oprah was just shaking her head. She handed me her journal and said, "Look for yourself."

I reached out and took from her the journal that she had with her while she was visiting God. I immediately began to read to myself what I saw contained upon those pages.

"My Daughters, My Sons, My Most Precious Children. Know that I am your God and your Father and it is through Moses once more that I speak to you all. It is time for my creation to once again return Home to Me.

1) Pray and meditate on your Loving Father. It is time for you to begin to seek me out.
2) Pray for the forgiveness of your sins. The greatest of these, being your failure to seek me out this lifetime and to put me above all things.
3) Pray to be counted as one of My own. My children will recognize my voice and know it to be true. My children are forever beings and will not perish, nor have they ever.
4) You will acknowledge My Son, Jesus Christ. That it is because of His perfect sacrifice that you were able to be

made whole once more and acceptable in My sight.

5) Choose to think good thoughts about yourself and others. For in doing so, you join with me in creation.
6) You will not be afraid of this time. I will remove from you the fear and in its place I will send you peace and love.
7) You are to pray for one another. For so doing, you are praying for yourselves. Your family and your neighbors ARE your Mothers, your Fathers, your sisters, your brothers, your children, your grandfathers and your grandmothers from life times gone by. I will place this knowing inside each and every one of you as Judgment Day approaches.
8) Any man or woman among you who gives to those who have not, will have redemption and earn a place in My Kingdom.
9) Be ready.
10) Sing, dance and be filled with Joy! Raise yourself up to Meet Me!

I looked up from what I had read on the pages of the journal that was resting in my lap and I just open mouthed stared at Oprah. I was lost for words. I just sat there and I said to Oprah.

“Well who knew?”

We both just howled. It could have been to just release some of the tension that we were both undoubtedly feeling.

“Wow, this is great!” I was in a state of surprise. I then added, “I mean it’s heavy. Really deep stuff. Oprah.” I paused. “Yeah. It is. But good, don’t you think?”

“Heck ya!”

Now it was my turn to be the reporter. The journalist.

"So, how long did it take you to get all of this?"

"About an hour and a half."

"Really? What was it like?"

"At first, it was slow, like I said, I was singing and breathing. I was noticing all the beauty around me. Then, I just picked up my pen and began to write down these knowings I was feeling. Honestly Sandra, at that point, It just poured out of me! Like, I was in this flow or something!"

I was glued to her every word.

"Then what?"

"Like you were saying, Sandra, I just got knowing after knowing and.." Oprah was snapping her fingers to demonstrate the speed at which she was receiving God's messages.

"Good job!" I congratulated her as I continued to look at her journal. Oprah leaned into me and we were both examining the writings together.
"

"It was very authoritative and commanding, just as you would expect God to be. No mincing words or sentiment. No room for discussion."

"Yeah, I got that too. Normally, this would of made me feel somewhat defiant, receiving all those orders. But Sandra, I know them to be true and it has left me with such a sense of peacefulness!"

"God has placed that into you Oprah, so you will know that it is real."

"I have to agree with you. Only, I imagine that there will be many views on this coming from different people." And here she took her index finger and tapped on the journal.

She continued to speak.

"I mean putting up a different set of commandments is going to spark controversy."

We both looked at one another. I responded to that concern with, "I guess that you could come from the fear about that. But look what it says in the third one." And I pointed it out to her.

"God's children will know it to be true." And we looked up at one another. I then said to her, "What are you worried about?"

Oprah shrugged her shoulders and then said, "I guess you're right. I mean, if history is gonna repeat itself again, I might as well surrender into this." And she breathed a heavy sigh "It worked out well the last time. It'll work out again now. You'll see."

"Maybe if I just carve it out on some of the big stones that you have laying around here."

I laughed at her great sense of humor.

"Very funny, coming from Moses over there!"

"Yeah, well, I guess it's happening again isn't it?"

"Same story, same characters. Different time and different names."

"You have to admit though, it does make sense that God would give us an updated version of things as times change. Trying to keep it familiar so that we could recognize it, yet different enough to be a test.

“Being a test” Oprah exclaimed and then said, “Why do you say a test, Sandra?”

I think that if you read up on the Bible, God is always giving us a test. A test to grade our faith.”

“Well, yeah, I can see that.”

“It really does make sense though, doesn't it. People's faith was tested time and time again in past generations, wouldn't it be fair to surmise that we could expect one as well?”

“Yeah. That does make perfect sense. Yeah, now that I am thinking on it.” Oprah sat up a little straighter and declared, “Come to think of it, this entire two days have been a test, haven't they Sandra?”

“Yes, Oprah, I guess in many ways, you're correct.”

“Well, think about it. God tested my faith when I decided to come up here and visit you Sandra.”

“How's that Oprah?”

“Well, after reading your book. I had such a strong knowing that I was to meet with you and relive what it was that was in your book. God tested my ability to hear His voice in you. Sandra, after spending this time with you, I not only can hear God's voice, and I mean I can literally hear God’s voice! I also am now knowing that He has this master plan for us all and having it spelled out to me, to us all through this journal” and she reached over and grabbed the book off my lap.

“In this work right here, this is faith. This is truth. This is the way towards God and this way will lead to a life of being one with God.”

I stood up on my feet and I began to applaud her.

"Wonderful, Oprah, wonderful. I think that you are ready to take on the world."

"Sandra, what am I to do with this? Do you think that God wishes for me to announce this?"

"I think that you have to ask yourself what it is that you are feeling you are to do? You know now it is God that truly guides everything in His creation. I would suggest you just "Be" with what you have received and wait for further instructions."

"Sandra," Oprah got up on her feet.

"I'm just so filled with this amazing energy right now that I can hardly contain how it is that I am feeling." She paused and then said, "You know what Sandra?" she asked but wasn't really asking me. She answered her own question.

"I think that I was to find Eckhart and to learn how it was to be present without the ego and without the labeling of things as either good or bad. I think I was to learn this from Eckhart so that when I read your book, I would be able to recognize it as an invitation to come up to your cottage. I mean, Sandra, I really could hear the voice of God directing me."

With that she stopped and then she turned and looked at me and she said, "Sandra, you're a gift. You're a gift from God and I am now just seeing for the first time how amazing that it is that you have come to know God, in this place and to be able to receive His word." And then she turned and faced the Garden and said in a voice not unlike a cheer, "And I have too!"

"Sandra, am I the first person that has ever been into the Garden to visit with God other than you?"

"No, I have told a few others before you that this is the Garden of Eden and I am met with blank stares. Pretty much what you would expect I guess. I know it does sound nuts to the average person. But to the spiritually enlightened individual, it's music to their ears!"

"Yes, because it is about discoveries made in the world of the spirit."

"You're right Oprah, discoveries of mine that until now have gone unknown. Hopefully, my book will change all of this and people will become more aware and want to build their own gardens and begin to have conversations with God."

"This could be a real fad. A new trend."

"Let's hope we can start something here because the good side of it is that we can help more people come to know the world of the spirit as they come to know God. Not just think of Him or dwell on Him."

Oprah butted in with, "Or memorize passages from the Bible."

"Or memorize passages from the Bible" I repeated and then continued, "Oprah, we can help people get really excited to know God and in turn, He will place His knowing of His plan for us inside each and every one of His children."

"Whatever way that He comes to you, be open because He comes to us all differently."

"Right. Today, God has come to me and spoken to me Sandra and I am amazed!"

"Well, Oprah, so am I."

With that, I got up and looked around and decided that with all of this excitement, it wouldn't hurt to have a swim before Doug and Gayle got here. I shared that thought with Oprah and she agreed.

“Sandra” Oprah’s face lost its smile and her tone became serious. She grabbed my wrist and ushered me back down onto the lounger. “Before we go for a swim, isn’t there still something you want to tell me first?”

My eyes popped wide open. A fear like that of being caught with my hand in the cookie jar sent chills up and down my spine. Like, what have I done wrong? Searching my mind wildly for what it could be, within seconds, Oprah alleviated my angst. Handing me her journal once again, she directed me.

“Turn the page and look at my final entry.”

I obeyed her instructions and tentatively began to turn the page.

Chapter Twenty-Nine

I began to read aloud.

"Sandra is to gather the names of my children who were present at the time of my Son's ascension. I have placed this knowing into my first Daughter Eve, the mother of My seed. Bring them all together upon the Mount of Olives in the month of December, the twenty-first day in the year 2012."

I looked up from the journal and directly into Oprah's eyes which were glaring at me demanding an explanation. I gave out a squeak of an "Oops!" I smiled sheepishly.

"Sandra, what on earth does this mean?"

I took in a breath and said, "Oprah I guess I have one more story to tell." She sat back down on her lounger and settled in while I poured myself another glass of lemonade. I sat down opposite her and began to unravel the mystery behind those words.

"A number of years ago, I was meditating and I was told by God that I was to get a book. Now this was confusing for me at first because I was writing books at the time and wondered did God mean that I am to write another book or 'get' a book?"

"So how did you figure out what it was that He meant?"

"Actually, it was just a few days afterwards that I received the answer. I was invited to visit my friend Rose, who by the way, in a past life time was Joseph, Christ's father."

I think by now Oprah was used to me blurting out these famous characters in history that were present during the time of Christ and remained dead-panned indicating that I was to just continue rather than wait for a reaction to this announcement. I began to elaborate.

“I was to be at Rose’s around nine o’clock Thursday morning. I arrived late because I got lost following the directions. Having located the correct destination, I was greeted at the house with a warm smiling welcome by Rose (My husband calls her ‘smiling Rose’ because she has this big white smile).” Oprah listened intently. I continued.

“She opened the door to me and immediately said that I was indeed meant to be there that day. I asked her ‘Why is that?’ and she shared with me that her phone rang at seven o’clock that morning and a man wanted to know if Sandra was there? I said to Rose, ‘Really?’ and she said to me ‘I guess that you are meant to be here today. Your coming was heralded.”

Oprah was staring at me and asked in that journalist tone of hers.

“So, you're telling me this man called out of the blue and asked for Sandra and this was a sign by God, the universe that you were being announced?”

“Well, yeah. So, I immediately was being clued into the fact that spirit was present with us and making itself known.”

“And you knew that because of what she had told you?”

“Yes. Because it was a strange coincidence.”

“And because there are no coincidences, everything happens for a reason, you naturally concluded God’s spirit was there?”

I agreed with that and told her, “I then handed Rose my coat and as we were proceeding into her family room, she suddenly turned to me and said, “Oh yeah, and there is one more thing. I am to buy you a book.” Oprah’s eyes flashed surprise.

"Oprah, I was stunned. I mean, I had just received information from God about a book and next thing you know it, God's intention was made crystal clear!"

"O.K. so did you then tell her about your mediation with God?"
"Yup. And the two of us sat down and tried to figure out God's intentions for this book."

"I remember telling her that I believed it was to be a book that could hold people's signatures."

"He told you that?"

"Well, yeah. I had a strong feeling about that and so did Rose."

"That is so amazing. So, what did you both decide to do?"

"Well, we both were no strangers to God's mysterious ways as we had a few adventures together with spirit in the early 2000's. So, we made no conclusions, except to remain open for spirit to bring Rose to the book."

"And did she?"

"Not for about six or seven months!"

"It took that long?"

"Yeah, and it was hard to wait. I kept asking God the entire time, 'When is the book coming?' and I got no answer."

"So eventually Rose got the book?"

"She did and do you know what?"

"What?"

“It was well worth the wait. Oprah, would you like me to show it to you?”

“You have it here with you? She was not able to contain her excitement.”

“Up here?”

“I always keep it close to me.” I assured her.

“Yes. Yes Sandra. I would love to see it!”

I instantly got up and went into the cottage to retrieve my treasured book. I returned within seconds and proudly presented it to Oprah upon my resurfacing from the cottage. She held out her hands and I placed it gently upon them after I had removed it’s cover. There was an immediate stillness that cocooned Oprah and I. A sense of awe incurred as she beheld the magnificent work of art. It was a brown leather bound book made in Italy.

“Where on earth did she find this?”

“At a store called Homesense.”

“Homesense?”

“Yeah. Which I seem to think was very appropriate considering this book is what is going to help us all go home to God.”

Oprah was not really listening now as she was caught up in the feelings that were being generated just by holding the book. I bent over and pointed out the beautiful relief picture that had been so wondrously crafted by the artist who had designed the book.

“Look at the three Goddesses that are on the book.”

"It is just so beautiful, Sandra." She said slowly as she began stroking the front cover.

"I know."

"

Who do you think is represented on the cover here?"

"I believe it to be Eve, The Virgin Mary and the Holy Grail Herself."

"Mary Magdalene?" she was quick to answer.

"Yes, I believe the three are as one."

Oprah had gone very quiet. I waited for a few minutes as she took in the energy of the book.

"Are you getting any special feelings or messages?"

"I am getting the word 'tablet'."

"Tablet." I echoed saying the word ever so slowly giving myself time to open up for any messages that I may be receiving on my end. Then suddenly spirit put into me, "Maybe it has something to do with the tablets you wrote upon as Moses?"

"Maybe."

"Maybe this book had the same energy in it that you felt when you held the tablets that contained the Ten Commandments and you recognize the energy as the energy of God?"

"Could be. I only know that I am breaking out in tingles all over the place and I feel like I could just float away. Sandra, what is this book for?"

She now had opened the book mid-way and beheld its contents.

"See, it has blank pages in it. And look Oprah, it's almost as if there are columns for people to sign their names on."

"I see that."

I decided to continue on with my story while she was examining the book.

"Anyway. Let me tell you the rest of the story. I then took the book to my friend Brenda, whom I mentioned earlier, the doctor of psychology." Oprah now looked up and began to pay attention once more to what I was telling her. I heard her utter, "Oh, yeah, I remember you mentioned her yesterday. So, go on."

"I went to her house with the specific intention to show her this book. I mean, after all, whenever something of this spiritual magnitude comes my way, I know enough to check in with her."

"Why her again?"

"Cause she does not channel spirit for anyone else except me."

"Go on" came the commandment.

"I was visiting with my other friend Karen which turned out to be a huge bonus because she was able to watch Brenda's young son while I showed the book to Brenda."

"You needed the peace and the quiet so that spirit could speak to you."

"You are getting very adept at this spiritual stuff my friend. Yes, that is correct. It is so important not to surround yourself with distractions when you are wishing for spirit to come in. So, Karen and Brenda's son went downstairs and Brenda and I were alone in the kitchen. I remember pulling the book out of the cover and placing it in her hands. And Oprah, what happened then was nothing and I mean nothing short of a miracle!"

"Tell me!"

"As soon as I had placed it into Brenda's hands she exclaimed to me. 'She found it! She found it! She found the book!' Now, I was quiet taken back by this comment from her and I said to Brenda. 'What do you mean?' Brenda then told me, 'We lost it. We lost it and she has found it!' Sandra, I have seen this book before. I don't know when and in what life time, but I know that we had this book before!"

Oprah's gaze was transfixed upon my face. I explained further.

"Oprah. I was wigging out at this! I mean I did not expect that reaction what so ever."

"Brenda then said. 'We tried to do this before, only we were stopped. We were being chased and we dropped it. I can see horses and a chase. We were riding for our lives and once it dropped into the mud, we could not go back for it or we would have lost our lives.' So, Oprah, I just stood there in her kitchen, with my mouth open and tried to figure out what was so important about this book, that having it in your possession resulted in a life threatening pursuit. And then it happened."

"What? What happened Sandra?"

"The most bizarre thing I have ever felt in my life. (Well, O.K. one of the most bizarre feelings I have ever had). Oprah, I can remember the feeling as clearly and as surely as if I were standing in that kitchen with her right this instant."

"What? Tell me!" I got up and proceeded to do a small demonstration.

"I held onto the book at the same time as Brenda did. All of a sudden I could sense this presence enter through the back door of the kitchen. It came up over Brenda's back, over her head and down her front. Then it entered into the book and up my hands, up over my front, over my head, and went down my back. Oprah! I exclaimed slowly. We were being covered in God's Holy Spirit! Oprah, God's Holy Spirit!"

Oprah sat in wide-eyed wonderment. I just got more and more excited as I continued to recant the incident.

"I then said to Brenda, 'Brenda, can you feel that?'"

"Yes she replied, smiling and just staring down at the book."

"Oh my God! This is amazing!" I said to her. I shut my eyes and began to breath in deeply, taking in as much of the energy as possible. I stopped for a short second to demonstrate to Oprah as I took the deepest breath that I could. Then opened my eyes and reported, "And Oprah, we were both riveted to the floor."

"Couldn't move again, eh?"

"Exactly, God's presence was among us and we were transfixed. It was a sacred moment." I paused for effect.

"It was a silent moment and we were both experiencing it together. Then, after about a minute or so of just standing there, unable to move, it began to leave."

"Just like that?" Oprah said.

"No. Slowly. As if it were being lifted from us." And I raised my palms to the sky to show her the direction that God's energy left us. Then added, "I opened my eyes and looked at my dear friend and said in slow motion.

"Oh my God!" Oprah, the smile on Brenda's face I will never

forget! I watched her open her eyes and look into mine. We were feeling the euphoria of having just been in the presence of God's Holy Spirit. Then slowly, we began to talk with one another. I let Brenda go first. She was holding and stroking the book.

"Sandra, this is really important. I mean, REALLY important."

"Ya think?" I answered.

She smiled and grew quiet, allowing her guides and angels to speak to her. As did I. Shortly, I whispered to her, "Brenda, I have been receiving in my meditations and channeling from God that this book is to be used for collecting signatures. I keep on getting the message 'five hundred'. I also keep getting that it has something to do with the Mount of Olives and Christ's ascension. Brenda looked up at me and said. 'Yes, yes I believe it does."

I asked her "What are you getting from it?"

Brenda just kept on stoking the book and finally said I think we started to do this before and now we are being asked to do it again. Collect the signatures of those who were there when Christ died or when He a rose up?"

"Ascended" We both said at the same time as spirit was now speaking to us both together."

I then turned to Oprah and said, "We put together the pieces from the images we received throughout the rest of the day and we figured it was around the time of King Arthur and The Round Table when we last tried to gather together the five hundred."

"You mean Lancelot, Lady Guinevere and Merlin the Magician? That time in history?"

"I believe so, Oprah. Only we were stopped short of our goal. Our sense was that this book and the signatures contained therein, are still known to us and we will remember them. Those people who have signed their names in it, will remember also."

Chapter Thirty

"You're saying that people are going to remember signing a book over five hundred years ago?"

"Longer than that."

"Whatever." And she lifted up her arm indicating she was not caring as she continued to expound upon her point.

"How are they going to remember signing a book that long ago, Sandra? Presuming that they can remember their past lives!"

"Oprah, I know it sounds outlandish. I know it sounds nuts. But they will remember. Their souls will remember and when they read about this in my book for you, they will know. They will know they are one of the souls that I seek."

"Oprah, I believe that God wants me to gather together the last five hundred souls that saw Christ alive. Those who witnessed His resurrected soul ascend into Heaven."

Now I could see by the expression upon the face of Oprah that her mind was hard at work. I am pretty sure that I had just given her lots to think about and she was taking her time formulating a question for me, but, for the moment, nothing was coming to the forefront. So, I said, "Think about it Oprah. Why else would God have given me the ability to know who people were from the time of Christ?"

Oprah put her hand to her mouth as she gasped.

"Oh my God! That's right Sandra. Your chart!"

"Yes. Now it is all starting to add up. Oprah, I have been charged with the task to gather those souls who were present when Christ ascended into Heaven. According to the Bible, the five hundred that were gathered together at the time of His Ascension."

"For what purpose Sandra?"

"Because I believe that those five hundred souls, each carry a piece of Christ that He left with them. Remember what I told you earlier about how to gain entrance into the Garden of Eden?"

"Huh?"

"In the Garden, eat the fruit, out of the Garden. In order to re-enter the Garden, follow it backwards to the beginning. Same rule applies here. Christ dwelt among us. Died. Resurrected. Ascended. If we want Him to return, we must provide the exact same environment that existed before He left."

"So, if the five hundred who were present then, were to come together in this lifetime?"

"Then we would be laying the foundation for His return." We both paused for a moment and allowed spirit to move us to the next question.

"So am I one of the five hundred?"

I smiled at that. She looked so cute. Like a little child asking for something from a loving parent.

I then asked her, "What do you think?"

She smiled back at me and said.

"I think yes."

I responded with, "I think yes too!" With that she grabbed a hold of the lounger and pulled herself forward.

"I am?"

"Yes, of course you are. Oprah, you have a big soul! An old historical soul. Your soul present on the earth indicates God's presence is dwelling amongst us in a big way!"

"I know that Sandra. But who was I then at the time of Christ?'
"I am seeing you as a woman covered in a black cloth over your head and body. I see you gathering up you daughter, who just happens to be Gayle."

"No! Really????? Gayle was my daughter?"

"Yes. And I see you looking out at an oncoming storm. As if you know that there is a storm brewing and you have to gather your child close to you and take cover."

"Really? And am I married?"

"You were. And you also had a son. But both your son and husband were killed and that is why I see you dressed in black. In fact, Oprah" I paused while I received the information, "The love you had for your husband that life time was so great that you swore you would never marry another and you carry that promise into this life time."

Oprah looked at me as if a light bulb had just lit up in her head.

"Really? So I am to sign the book and Gayle too?"

"That is correct."

"But how do you know for sure Sandra who is to sign and who is not."
"Remember this Oprah. I know nothing. It is God who knows and it is God that puts the knowing into me."

"Oh my God Oprah, I just asked universe who was your son at the time of Christ. Oprah, it was Mattie. Oprah! It was Mattie!!!!!!"

I had taken Oprah by surprise. The look upon her face was that of a person being washed over by God's heavenly knowing as she drew in a breath and held onto it for a short second. Her hand went immediately to her mouth. The tears began to well up in her eyes and gently began to make their way slowly down Oprah's cheeks.

"Oh Sandra!" she gasped."

I also began to well up with tears. I could also feel the energy and the emotion that was now so strong in the air. It was joy, it was God revealing Himself once more to us both. We shone with recognition of His universal truth.

Then Oprah and I both just sobbed with knowing. I think for Oprah there was a huge energetic release and we just sat and allowed ourselves to be in this miraculous moment. She broke the silence as she held out here arm to me and said.

"Oh Sandra, I am covered in goose bumps!"

"Me too my friend. Me too! I am tingling from head to toe. Let me just go and grab some Kleenex."

With that I jumped up and quickly went inside the cottage to retrieve a box. I brought it outside immediately and handed the box out to Oprah. She took two and began to dry her eyes.

"Oh Sandra, that makes so much sense. He was such a smart little boy and I loved him instantly!"

"Now you know it was because He used to actually be your own son at the time of Jesus."

"Yes."

"A prophet."

Again Oprah's face lit up with recognition of a truth being realized. "Yes. A prophet, Sandra! He was so young and yet so wise for his young years."

"Like his mother."

Oprah looked at me and smiled at the heart-felt compliment.

"Yes, like his Mother two thousand years ago."

"Oprah, we come around to one another again and again."

"Sandra, it all seems to make so much sense. How is it that we can have life everlasting if we haven't already had it?"

"Exactly Oprah. Exactly. We all are forever beings. Our souls are that of God's and He is now and will be forever."

"Just as we are!"

"Yes."
"So, Sandra..." Oprah said as she put her Kleenex down. "What we are talking about here is God's desire for us to bring back His Son to walk amongst us once more."

"Yes, I believe that it is our goal."

"So, according to the Bible then, these are the end of days. And now with this revelation you have just presented me with, which is fascinating. I mean, if God is asking you to do this for Him, and He is placing the knowing inside of you, well. Perhaps it is time for us all to help you find the five hundred souls that you seek."

"I actually feel that if we, all the Christians of the world, as the body of Christ, decide to see this thing through. Well, I believe that we can, as a collective consciousness experience the second coming of Christ on December 21st 2012."

"And it is that day because?"

"It's what I am being told is the date to do this on."

"That date lines up with the Mayan Calendar."

"Yes, I am aware of that."

"So you think that you can find in the next few years, all the right five hundred signatures?"

"I think with God's help I can. And that is correct of you to emphasis that Oprah."

"What?"

"It has to be the right five hundred people present. Why do you think that is Sandra?"

"It has to do with Christ leaving a piece of Himself inside each those five hundred souls."

"Like all the pieces have to come together in order to have the whole picture."

"Exactly."

"Well girlfriend, count me in! Now where is a pen?" I immediately jumped up and handed her a pen that I had placed on the patio table. Oprah took a moment and turned to the front of the book. Here she made the observation that several signatures had already been entered into the book.

"Oh look, there is Brenda's signature, and Karen's." She looked up at me puzzled. "And here is Jesus' name in your handwriting Sandra. Why is that?"

"Not sure yet, Oprah. I was just guided to write that."

"And what about all these people here?"

"Well, I think that my next book should be about the lives of the five hundred whose names are entered into the book."

"Why is that?'

"Cause it is a pretty good story surrounding my first collection of signatures." Oprah just gave me the look that said. 'Do I really have to ask you?"

I smiled and quickly said in a teasing manner, "Well it I give away all my good stories now, what will be left for my next book?" and I smiled a very broad smile.

I gave in far too quickly.

"Oh alright then. It was Christmastime and all the characters whom were present at this party were also present at the time of Christ's birth. I mean, I just could feel it and every time I turned around that night, people were coming up to me and I knew instantly whether or not they were a shepherd, or a wise man. It was so wild that I left the party and drove all the way home to get the book and drove all the way back to the party to obtain people's signatures."

"You mean in the middle of a party, you told people, strangers even that they had to sign your book????"

"Yes. I did that."

"What balls you have, girlfriend!! What did people say to you?"

"Well that's the interesting part. Most people signed it without a second thought. One man, whom I had never met in my life or seen since, I think he designs airplanes. Anyways, he told me upon signing that I am not the only person who thinks this way! It made me feel not so alone."

Looking at the book she commented to me, "Looks like a high school year book!"

"Yeah. I thought so too. I was hoping people would sign their names in the columns provided. But, hey! My angel friend tells me that it does not matter, just as long as they sign it."

"Where would you like me to sign it Sandra?"

"Anywhere that you feel moved to sign Oprah."

After hearing those instructions, she choose a page and placed upon it my first famous person's signature. Famous in this lifetime that is! I then took the book from her and thanked her for the honor. I beheld her name in big bold print. Smiled. Then I closed the book, returned it to its cover, turned and went inside the cottage. After I had placed it back in a safe place. I rejoined my guest, who by the way, this time was just getting up and giving herself a good long stretch.

"Are you ready for a swim now?"

"Yes. That would be marvelous!" Oprah smiled at me and then came over and took both my hands in hers. She stared deep into my eyes what seemed like a very long time. She then took in a breath and said something that I never expected.

"Sandra, this time it is I who would like to say a prayer." I was silenced by this announcement, yet humbled. I smiled and then with my head bowed I waited to hear her blessing.

"Heavenly Lord, our loving Father whom has seen fit to bless us this weekend with many a miracle and many a revelation. We give heart-felt thanks for this time, Sandra and I have so lovingly shared with one another. I would ask you now Lord, to watch over my friend and to keep close to her. Please Father, guide her safely along the path that you have laid out for her and send your mightiest of angels to keep close watch over her. Bring safely to Sandra those of your children that carry with them a piece of our Savior. For it is within them, the five hundred souls who witnessed Christ's ascension that lay the "Official Hope of The World." We ask that you allow the task at hand to come to fruition with grace and ease. And that may all of your children, God, return safely Home to You. We thank you now for the great whether, the great food and the wonderful company of these past few days. In Jesus' name we pray. Amen."

I opened my eyes and reached out and immediately gave Oprah a loving hug.

After we embraced, it seemed like quite awhile before we both let go of one another and stood, still holding hands, smiling into one another's face, reflecting back our love for one another.

"Let's go swimming!"

Chapter Thirty-One

We both got on our suits and had a quick swim in the lake. By the time we had finished, and headed up to the cottage to change I could hear the familiar sound of a car horn announcing my son's arrival. Oprah and I walked around to the back of the cottage just in time to see the car pulling up in the lane. The door opened and Gayle popped her head out and announced, "We're here. We're here!"

I turned to Oprah and whispered, "Thanks for the great adventure Oprah.

"No, thank-you Sandra. It was more than I could have hoped for in a million years. No, literally."

We both snickered and then turned and headed towards the new arrivals.

I looked up and saw that wonderful little smile on my son's face and I could tell that all went well. That the trip had gone smoothly and that he too had enjoyed Gayle's company.

Oprah went to embrace Gayle and I did the same to my son.

"Have a good ride did you, Dougie?"

"Yes Mom. Gayle and I really go to know everything there was to know about each other."

"That's nice. Are you hungry? Would you like something to eat?"

"Yes, I think I'll jump in the lake and have a swim first and then I'd love a hamburger or something!"

"I must have read your mind."

I could hear Oprah and Gayle chatting and exchanging pleasantries, “Gayle, are you up for a swim?” I offered.

“Yes, I stopped and bought a suit when your son Doug told me that is probably what I would want to do once I got here.”

“Well yeah, he's right. It helps to wash the trip off of you!”

“Sandra” Oprah called me over.

“Sandra, this is my good friend, Gayle.”

Gayle glared at her. Oprah caught herself and then corrected her statement. “I'm sorry, my best friend, Gayle.” We all laughed.

“It's a pleasure to meet you at last Gayle. I am very grateful to you for allowing me the company of your buddy here for the past day or so.”

“Well, Sandra, after speaking to Oprah on the phone last night, I am thinking that it is I who should be thanking you!”

“I am pleased to have gotten such a good report. Now if you ladies will follow me up to the cottage.” With that we turned around and headed towards the cottage. I continued on “Oprah, you take Gayle and show her around. Maybe you could share your room so that she has a place to change and then while you both are having a swim, I'll get some food on the grill.”

“Sounds like a plan” Gayle pipes in, then adds, “Oprah, can I see the Garden?”

Oprah just looks at me and I look at her and I say, “Well, that will be up to her Majesty.”

Gayle turns to Oprah and says, “Yeah, I heard about that majesty thing. Let's hear more about that!”

“It'll be great conversation for the long ride back to the airport Gayle. We have a lot of time to put in and luckily, I have the story to do it!”

We all laughed.

I quickly prepared dinner and we ate as soon as everyone had finished their swim and had gotten changed into some warmer clothes. It cools down in the evening at the cottage.

After we finished eating, it didn't take too long before Doug announced that he wanted to get going on the road before it got dark. The girls complied and Oprah went inside to pack. Gayle and I were alone on the patio. I turned to her and said. “Oprah is so lucky to have such a good friend in you, Gayle.”

“Why thank-you Sandra.”

“I know that she loves you very much.”

“You don't have to tell me twice, Sandra. You know in many ways, she is just like a sister or a mother to me. Know what I mean?”
“
I know exactly what you mean Gayle. Exactly what you mean!” I couldn’t help but laugh to myself at that one!

“Sandra, this meant a lot to Oprah to come up here. She was fairly nervous about it too!"”

“Really?”

“Oh yeah. She wasn't quite sure what to make of all of this.”

“Well, I will be anxious to hear back from her after she has had a chance to digest some of the information she received in these past forty-eight hours."

"Oh, if I know Oprah, and I do, she will most likely be getting back to you!"

"I will look forward to that."

"I hope that sometime I will be invited to come up to the Garden as well."

"That could be a possibility, although, you can build your own you know."

"I can?"

Oh yeah, Oprah will tell you how."

"Good enough."

With that Oprah appeared at the cottage back door and I smiled up at her. "Well, it looks as though you're packed and ready to go!"

""'She made her way over to give me a most lovely hug. Oprah squeezed me and as she did she whispered into my ear. "I will always remember this time. It was magical!

"Yes, truly it was" I whispered back.

"Take care, Eve."

"You too, Moses."

We broke apart and held hands and lovingly stared into one another's eyes.

"May God Bless you and keep you in His care Oprah."
"And you as well. Thank-you!"

"You're so very welcome!"

We stood and smiled at one another and I offered to walk them to the car. Douglas had taken their things and placed them in the trunk of the car and was waiting with the door held for Oprah.

"It has been one heck of a ride, has it not?"

"Yes Sandra, one heck of a ride."

"Now if you have any questions or anything that you would think that I would find interesting, do not hesitate to call me." With that I held out a paper that contained my name and phone number. E-mail as well.

"I will put this in my bag, Sandra."
Doug, very graciously moved the ladies into the car with a grand hand gesture, "Ladies"

"I will be in touch Sandra." Oprah hugged me one more time and said "Thank-you!" I smiled in return, as I broke our embrace.

Oprah and Gayle got into the car and Doug closed the doors. "Now you both enjoy the ride and go easy on Doug. O.K.?"

"Mom" Doug assured me, "I can handle them."

I winked at my son and I said to him, say hi to Dad for me and tell him to call me later on tonight."

"O.K. Mom, see ya!"

"Bye hon. I kissed him and he got into the driver's seat.

He backed the car out and all three of them waved good-bye. As they pulled away I stood in the drive, waving until they were almost out of sight. I deployed my angels all around them for a safe ride home and I turned once they were out of sight and I began to walk back towards the cottage.

As I was crossing the lawn, I happened to glance over towards the Garden. You could see past the Garden and into the water. The sun was beginning to set and the sky was pink and purple. I felt the peace and the calm of the evening air and I wrapped my arms around my shoulders and half said to myself and half said into the Garden as I looked up into the tree tops, "Thy will be done, Oh Wonderful Lord Father God. Thy will be done."

The End

13222093R00139

Made in the USA
Charleston, SC
24 June 2012